License, Disclaimer of Liability, and Limited Warranty

Adobe Flash® Animation

Creative Storytelling for the Web and TV

Philip Carrera

JONES & BARTLETT
L E A R N I N G

World Headquarters

Jones & Bartlett Learning
40 Tall Pine Drive
Sudbury, MA 01776
978-443-5000
info@jblearning.com
www.jblearning.com

Jones & Bartlett Learning
Canada
6339 Ormindale Way
Mississauga, Ontario L5V 1J2
Canada

Jones & Bartlett Learning
International
Barb House, Barb Mews
London W6 7PA
United Kingdom

Jones & Bartlett Learning books and products are available through most bookstores and online booksellers. To contact Jones & Bartlett Learning directly, call 800-832-0034, fax 978-443-8000, or visit our website, www.jblearning.com.

Substantial discounts on bulk quantities of Jones & Bartlett Learning publications are available to corporations, professional associations, and other qualified organizations. For details and specific discount information, contact the special sales department at Jones & Bartlett Learning via the above contact information or send an email to specialsales@jblearning.com.

Production Credits
Publisher: David Pallai
Acquisitions Editor: Timothy McEvoy
Editorial Assistant: Molly Whitman
Production Director: Amy Rose
Senior Production Editor: Katherine Crighton
Senior Marketing Manager: Andrea DeFronzo
Associate Marketing Manager: Lindsay Ruggiero
V.P., Manufacturing and Inventory Control: Therese Connell
Composition and Project Management: Northeast Compositors, Inc.
Cover Design: Scott Moden
Cover and Title Page Image: © Philip Carrera
Printing and Binding: Malloy, Inc.
Cover Printing: Malloy, Inc.

Library of Congress Cataloging-in-Publication Data
Carrera, Philip.
  Adobe Flash animation : creative storytelling for the web and TV / Philip Carrera.
     p. cm.
  ISBN-13: 978-0-7637-8415-7
  ISBN-10: 0-7637-8415-X
  1. Computer animation. 2. Flash (Computer file) 3. Video recordings--Production and direction. 4. Digital video. I. Title.
  TR897.7.C387 2011
  006.6'96--dc22   2010011044

6048
Printed in the United States of America
14 13 12 11 10   10 9 8 7 6 5 4 3 2 1

CONTENTS

Preface   xi

Who This Book Is For   xii

Acknowledgments   xii

CHAPTER 1   WHAT'S THE BIG IDEA?   1
Finding Inspiration   1
Where to Begin   1
Personal Experience   3
Get Out There   5
Characters   6
Visual Storytelling   6
Summary   7
Exercises   7

CHAPTER 2   SET YOURSELF UP   9
Equipment   9
Workflow   12
Organization   16
File Preparation   17
Your Workspace   20
Summary   23
Exercises   23

CHAPTER 3   GET THE LEAD OUT   27

Applying Traditional Principles in the Digital Realm   27
Setting Your Preferences   27
Keyboard Shortcuts   31
Program Interface   34
Drawing   36
Some Drawing Principles   36
Drawing in Adobe Flash   40
Working with Color   54
Gradients   55
Advanced Shapes   57
Layering   59
Importing a Bitmap   60
Transform Tools   62
Summary   64
Exercises   64

CHAPTER 4   THE WRITE STUFF   67

Brainstorming a Concept   67
Using a Story to Promote   67
Using Your Story to Teach   68
Using Your Story to Present   69
Elements of a Story   70
Characters   70
Plot   72
The Script   74
Summary   82
Exercises   82

CHAPTER 5   IF YOU BUILD IT, THEY WILL COME   85

Visual Development   85
Research   86
Character Design   87
Background Design   90
Use Reference   92
Two-Dimensional Composition and Design   93
Background Layout   98
Reusing Backgrounds   98

Staging   99
Camera   109
Continuity   110
Pacing   110
Color Theory   111
Color Meanings   111
Color Palette and Mood   112
Assembling a Library   114
Character Rigging via Symbols   117
Layering Body Parts   118
The Eight-Point Turnaround   119
The Model Sheet   122
Expression Sheets   123
Textures   124
Summary   133
Exercises   133

CHAPTER 6   WHAT YOU SEE IS WHAT YOU GET   135
The Storyboard   135
Shot Composition   138
The Animatic   139
Timing in Adobe Flash   143
Camera Movements in Adobe Flash   144
Camera Cut   144
Camera Shake   145
Camera Twist   146
Rack Focus   148
The Cross Dissolve   149
Fade to Black   149
Truck In   150
Pan Across   150
Pan Up   151
Parallax Effect   151
Iris In/Out   151
Wipe   154
Sound   154
Sound Editing in Adobe Flash   156
Summary   157
Exercises   157

CHAPTER 7   SHOW AND TELL   159

Animation   159
Twelve Principles of Animation   160
Walk Cycle   166
Rough Animation   167
The Motion Tween with Rotation   168
Shape Tween   169
Motion Guide   169
Nesting Symbols   171
Animating Dialogue   176
Special Effects   177
Creative Title and Credits Design   177
Project 1: Steampunk   177
Project 2: 70's Disco   190
Project 3: Neon Glow   194
Project 4: Freezing Ice   197
Project 5: Moving Light   201
Project 6: Down in Flames   204
Project 7: Light Burst   210
Project 8: Mask Reveal   214
Project 9: Electricity   220
Project 10: Melting Blob   224
Summary   227
Exercises   228

CHAPTER 8   SHARING IS CARING   229

Preparation for Delivery   229
Optimization   229
Exporting from Adobe Flash   238
Editing Your Clips   241
Promotion and Marketing   242
Networking   242
Distribution   243
Film Festivals   244
Online Contests   245
Summary   245
Exercises   245

CHAPTER 9   ONE-ON-ONE WITH THE PROS   247

Q & A with Linda Simensky, Vice President of Children's
Programming, PBS   247
Q & A with James Reitano, Creative Director, TFU
Studios   250
Q & A with Bob Harper   252
Q & A with Sam Chi   253
Q & A with Barney Saltzberg   255
Q & A with Jeff Zikry   256
Q & A with Dave Redl, Familypants.com   259
Q & A with Wyatt Miles   263

Index   267

PREFACE

Whether huddled around a campfire, hammering chisel to stone, or putting pen to paper, humans have been telling stories for thousands of years. Though the elements of a good story have remained the same, how we share them has evolved with every passing generation. There was a time when reaching an audience larger than a group of family and friends would require the coordinated effort of several people and a great deal of negotiation and compromise. Today, advancements in technology give you the power to singlehandedly write, design, animate, and distribute your story to a global audience from the comfort of your own home in a fraction of the time. My goal is to show you how to do just that using Adobe® Flash® software.

Assuming you have no prior knowledge of the software, I will take you step by step through the process of telling your story; whether it's an original pilot for television, a visual accompaniment to your sales presentation, or countless other possibilities, this book contains everything you need. All that's required from you is your imagination and a determination to see your vision come true.

We will begin by exploring the many opportunities that exist for storytelling—from the classroom to the boardroom—and where inspiration lies, waiting to be revealed. Equipped with an idea, we will delve into the many tools that Flash places at your disposal. Rather than attaining the "style" that has made Flash so easily recognizable, you will see that like any other media, when Flash is used as a tool, the possibilities for what your story could look like are infinite. To accomplish this, we will cover several principles of animation, character and background design, and cinematography. How you apply these principles will determine the look and feel of your story.

In essence, this book is like a miniature classroom in your hands. Designed as a textbook, each chapter concludes with a brief summary highlighting its most important principles, as well as hands-on practice exercises, that can help you see your story unfold as you progress through the book. An accompanying DVD contains original Flash files that you can dissect and compare with your own. To further enhance your learning experience, the DVD includes recorded video tutorials of more complex lessons that you can follow at your own pace.

Lastly, we'll wrap up the book by exploring several avenues for promotion and distribution, including using the Internet as your promotional tool. The larger your audience, the more feedback you'll get. And isn't sharing your story the reason you made it in the first place? So let's get started. Your audience awaits.

WHO THIS BOOK IS FOR

This book is for students of animation, new media, and film as well as working professionals looking to produce an independent film, pitch a television show, or create animated shorts for the web, presentations, lectures, or classrooms.

ACKNOWLEDGMENTS

Toni Morrison once said, "If there's a book you really want to read, but it hasn't been written yet, then you must write it." When I began learning the craft of visual storytelling, I read lots of books, attended many classes, scoured the internet, and soaked up every bit of information I could get my hands on, all the while wishing, "If only there were just one book that I could turn to whenever I had a question or needed inspiration."

That book didn't exist, but along the way, I've been blessed with many people who have either challenged me, inspired me, or lent me a helping hand to create this book. In chronological order, they are Victor Carrera, Deirdre Lashgari, Jim Laris, Mike Whitlow, my third grade students at Workman Elementary, Don Sciore, Agnes Carrera, Tim Pixton, Blake Caldwell, Dean Caruso, and Gary Oliverio.

I also extend my sincerest gratitude to Molly Whitman and Tim McEvoy of Jones & Bartlett for their guidance and patience. Thanks to them, that book now exists. And finally, thanks to all of my Flash animation students over the years. Their enthusiasm and spirit is what inspired me to write this book. Though many of them have moved on toward fulfilling careers in animation, I hope this book helps up-and-coming storytellers for many generations to come.

Chapter 1 · What's the Big Idea?

"Life itself is the most wonderful fairy tale of all."
—Hans Christian Andersen

FINDING INSPIRATION

Everywhere you look, stories animated in Flash are being told. Science museums commonly use Adobe® Flash® technology to create animated interactive displays to teach everything from how gears and pulleys work, to the history of flight. Courtrooms now include animated presentations that help attorneys visually build their cases with their juries: to show the profits and losses of a corrupt corporation, for example. Elementary schools utilize Adobe Flash in everything from interactive books to videos on how to behave during a fire drill. On any given day, you can drive by an animated billboard promoting the latest laundry detergent or sports drink. As long as people have something to say, stories will be told, and animation will always be at the heart of storytelling because it's something we've grown up enjoying. The familiarity we share with this medium is what makes it so successful. Now, with the ubiquity of portable media players and podcasting, animated stories that are created using Adobe Flash are more popular than ever.

WHERE TO BEGIN

So, where will you find your ideas? For starters, try looking at the things that interest you. Perhaps there is an old fairy tale that you've always enjoyed. Try

FIGURE 1-1   Characters designed and animated using Adobe® Flash® technology.

reinterpreting it with different types of characters or placing it in a completely different setting. Consider telling it from a different point of view. Think back to a joke you heard that could be even funnier if it was translated visually. Place it in a different time period, and see what that does to the story. Try drawing what you imagine a character from your favorite book to look like, and give that character a new name. Then make up a story about it. The same can be done with the description of a location. The key is to embellish the drawing with your own added touches, like adding a bird fountain where none was before. Stretch yourself even further creatively by deciding that the bird fountain looks nothing like any bird fountain you've ever seen. The further away you go from your comfort zone, the more ideas you'll have. This includes seeing films you normally wouldn't consider, reading magazines that have never caught your eye,

FIGURE 1-2   Imagine a conversation taking place. What are they talking about?

exploring a section in your local library you never knew existed. Even taking a different route home could lead to a story you otherwise would have missed out on.

PERSONAL EXPERIENCE

Often stories can be found right where you are: a conversation you overheard on the train, an interesting person you saw on the street, a funny interaction between a pigeon and a squirrel in the park. The key is to actively look.

It helps to have a notebook handy in which jot down any thoughts that come to mind, too. Take some time to sketch whatever catches your eye. You may learn something about it you've never noticed before. No time to sketch? Snap a picture. Turn it into a series of photographs. Something as simple as a city bus looks very different in the Philippines than it does in New York.

FIGURE 1-3   Where could this doorway lead?

GET OUT THERE

Traveling to far away places is a great way to find inspiration for new stories. If that's not an option, study new cultures by learning another language or by trying a new restaurant. Every part of the world has its own theater, music, food, and fashion. As a storyteller, you should make it your hobby to learn about them.

Armed with all this knowledge, try writing a poem. The great Chilean poet Pablo Neruda wrote an entire book consisting of odes to everyday things. You could write about something as mundane as waking up in the morning, and you could turn it into a wonderful adventure. The next time you're out grocery shopping, try to imagine what it would be like if all the produce came alive after business hours. Quite a few feature films have been made based on a similar concept. The important thing is that you write a story about something you're passionate about. Maybe there is a cause that is close to your heart. The reason documentaries are so moving is that the directors feel deeply connected to the subjects they're revealing. The more you care about your story, the more your audience will empathize. That's not to say that you should be writing with an audience in mind. On the contrary, the story you tell should be one that you believe needs to be told and one that only you can tell. Your story will naturally find an audience, because regardless of where people come from, humans share certain universal traits. We all know what it's like to feel a need, desire, disappointment, joy, hope, hopelessness, accomplishment, and despair. The reason we never want the mean ol' cat to catch the cute little mouse is because it's our nature to root for the underdog.

FIGURE 1-4   Use your imagination. How does this character feel? Why?

CHARACTERS

Once you have a rough idea and some players in mind, get to know your characters by developing a back story for each of them. How old are they? Where did they come from? What are their likes and dislikes? How do they dress? What kind of education do they have? Do they have any quirks or physical characteristics worth noting? When professional actors are preparing for a role, they zero in on the most minute details of a character, sometimes even down to how the character walks, or if they are partial to a certain type of candy. The more you offer your character at this stage, the more pleasantly surprised you'll be when your character does something unexpected at the later stages of preparing your script. It's quite common for a writer to describe his characters in the third person when discussing the writing process because they truly come alive as the story unfolds.

VISUAL STORYTELLING

For your audience to care about your story, you need to pull the viewer out of their reality and into your world. As a result, believability in your characters and their setting is crucial. To achieve this, you must think visually. For example, if the opening frame is a still shot in the park, think of little details you could add to make it more believable: a flock of birds flying by in the distance, or some autumn leaves meandering across the scene. Details like these can immediately give the viewer a sense of what time of year it is. The design of the nearby buildings or fencing around the park can make the difference between it being an English garden in the Victorian era, or a modern day park in Phoenix, Arizona.

Your characters should be approached the same way. If a character is sitting alone in the dentist's lobby, have him tap his foot nervously, chew his fingernails, or watch a small spider rappelling in the corner. These small moments in time provide insight into your character and how he feels about his situation, all without saying a word. The fact that the character happens to be a robot just adds to the humor of the scene. At the same time, we sympathize with him because we can all relate to the anxiety of waiting for the dreaded moment when our name is called. Remember, the more the viewer recognizes himself in your character, the more his interest will be retained.

SUMMARY

In this chapter, we discussed many of the ways animation could be used to tell a story, and the importance of being a proactive story seeker. Tips for finding new stories included: carrying a notebook to jot down ideas, sketching objects or places that spike your interest, finding a cause or topic that interests you, and experiencing new things to fuel your creativity. We also covered two vital elements to your story: setting and character, and one approach to telling your story with added richness: thinking visually. The more time and effort you devote to this exploratory stage, the more fun you'll have developing the idea and refining the story later on.

EXERCISES

Exercise 1.1

Go to a café, the park, or the beach, and watch the people interact around you. Write down what you think their occupations are, what their hobbies are, and give them fictitious names, like Cornelius Knickerbocker III, or Sardinia Lilyflower. Note their body gestures and try to guess what they're talking about, what they're thinking. Ask yourself what their homes look like. What kinds of pets do they have? The more outlandish your answers, the more fun your stories will be.

Exercise 1.2

Look around your home, or go outside and make inanimate objects come alive by drawing them with anthropomorphic qualities. What would a tree look like if it uprooted itself and decided to run down the street? What does a mailbox coughing up letters look like? What if an elementary school sprouted wings? What would a conversation between a cloud and a sailboat out at sea look like?

Chapter 2   SET YOURSELF UP

"If I had eight hours to chop down a tree, I'd spend six sharpening my axe."

—Abraham Lincoln

EQUIPMENT

The beauty of animation lies in its inherent ability to tell a story with whatever media you choose. Throughout history, stories have been animated with sand, clay, paper cutouts, salt, paint on glass, pencil and paper, chalk on slate, and a myriad of other media. Works of art like these, as beautiful as they are, are very time-consuming and can be quite expensive to do.

The digital age has made animation much more accessible due to the affordability of computers and their peripherals. One peripheral you definitely want in your possession also happens to be a standard in today's animation studios. It's the digital tablet and stylus.

There was a time when storyboard artists drew all of their panels by hand and passed them off to a production assistant, who then had the laborious task of scanning each sheet into the computer, assigning each scan an appropriate filename for sequencing, and then importing and arranging each scene in Flash. Now, you can draw your storyboards, character designs, model sheets, and backgrounds completely using Adobe® Flash®, foregoing that entire process. If you've never used a tablet and stylus, you may experience a slight learning curve, but don't let that discourage you. Once you grow accustomed to drawing with it, you'll wonder how you ever managed without one.

FIGURE 2-1   Illustration of a digital tablet and stylus.

Another necessity is a portable hard drive. There are many to choose from, ranging in sizes from 100 GB to 1 TB (terabyte), and they can be as large as a hardcover book or small enough to fit in your pocket. Find one with a USB connection that is compatible with both Mac and PC, because you never know when you may need to transfer a file onto another computer for testing or simply share a file. Remember to back up your work at the end of each day. There's nothing worse than losing your work due to a sudden power outage or computer crash and not having a file backup.

Poor sound quality in a film can be a distraction, rendering it unwatchable. Invest in a good desktop microphone that can easily be plugged into your computer. These can range in cost anywhere from $20 to $100. Good microphones have built-in noise-cancelling features to help reduce background noise. If, during playback, you hear pops and hisses, try attaching a pop filter to the microphone. That should help minimize unwanted sounds. If you're working from home, test it out in different rooms before going too deep into production to ensure you're getting the sound quality you want. Preferably, you

FIGURE 2-2   Illustration of a couple of microphones with a USB connector.

will want a room that is carpeted and with few windows to minimize any echo during the recording process.

A good audio-editing program can help enhance your recording by offering you the ability to adjust volume and pitch. Several programs are offered online for free or can be purchased for a reasonable fee. Here's a list of some user-friendly programs worth exploring: Audacity®, Sound Forge Audio Studio®, Garageband®, and iMovie®. Your PC will probably already have programs like Sound Recorder® and Moviemaker® installed. For some projects, that may be all you need. Whichever editing software you choose, make sure your audio files can be converted to either a .wav file (native to PCs), an .aif file (native to Macs), or an .mp3 file (cross platform). Depending on your operating system, you'll be working with one of these three audio file types in your animation project.

Just as you'll be editing your sound, you will also be editing your scenes. Although video-editing programs have varying levels of complexity, for a small project (under 5 minutes with little to no special effects), programs like Moviemaker (free for PCs) or iMovie (free for Macs) should work just fine. The larger and more sophisticated your project, however, the more you'll appreciate more robust programs like After Effects® (available for PC and Mac), or Final Cut Pro® (Mac).

WORKFLOW

A lot goes into a production. Understanding the steps involved can save you from realizing midway through the animation stage that an entire scene was not accounted for in the animatic. If it had, you would have known that the main character had changed costumes prior to entering your scene. To help you avoid backtracking and to ensure that you stay on track, here is an overview of the production process.

1. *Idea*
   As discussed in Chapter 1, this is where it all begins. Having a strong concept you believe in will carry you through the arduous process of making a film. The more progress you make, the more excited you'll be as you see your idea come to fruition.

2. *Script*
   The script will serve as your blueprint as you develop the story. In addition to containing the dialogue and scene descriptions, you will also want to include camera movements, transitions, and emotional cues to describe how a character may be feeling at that moment. These details will help you later as you prepare the animatic. Often, directors will thumbnail shots or scribble notes in the margins for later reference.

3. *Visual Development*
   With script in hand, you will begin designing a mood for your film. This involves determining a color palette and creating concept art that can serve as inspiration when designing your characters and backgrounds. The visual development stage is your opportunity to experiment with different styles and camera angles. Play with different media: colored pencils, watercolor, pastels, and/or acrylic paints. If you're more comfortable with digital media, customize your own brushes in Adobe® Photoshop®, or layer and distort photographs to make collages. Use a combination of both digital paint and collage. Think of this as your artistic playground.

4. *Character Design/Model Sheets*
   By the time you reach this stage, you will most likely already have an idea of what you want your characters to look like. The observational skills you developed when sketching people on location will help you here. Focus on simple, overall shapes to establish characters' postures. Are they rounded? Angular? How would you show a character who is proud versus one who lacks confidence? How does a cranky, bitter spinster differ from a fun-loving, carefree aristocrat? When preparing each character's model

sheet, open up their silhouettes so it's clear what they are doing and how they are feeling. Show them experiencing different emotions: overjoyed, frightened, determined, overwhelmed. Photographic references can be used for costumes as well.

5. *Storyboard*

The storyboard is a visual interpretation of the script. Its purpose is to determine staging (where characters stand in relation to one another and the objects with which they interact), blocking (where the camera is in relation to the characters), posing (a character's body gestures to best express their feelings and most clearly tell their story), camera movements (cuts, pans, truck in/out), transitions (wipes, dissolves), and to break down scenes (what the viewer sees and hears at any given time). Your storyboards can be as detailed as you need them to be; they will be your initial guide to visualizing your film.

6. *Voice Record*

Now that you know what your characters look like and how they will interact, giving them a voice will come more naturally. You could try recording some voices yourself, but you may be better off asking your friends to help. An accent can do wonders to bring a character to life, so try faking one if you can do it convincingly. The more people you have to choose from, though, the better. Every actor should have a copy of your script, and if only one microphone is available, you will want each actor to run through his/her lines from beginning to end so the flow is not disrupted. Be sure to add some silence after each paragraph, so you'll have room to trim the audio clips later. Since the film is animated, there's no need for your actors to memorize their lines, but some preparation is always helpful. Avoid flat, monotone readings, unless it's intentionally written that way to contrast with the visual. Your actors should "act" not "read" their lines. Sometimes, the more your actors exaggerate their delivery, the more creative you can be when animating your character. This ability to defy reality is what separates animation from live action.

7. *Animatic*

Now that you have your storyboards and audio clips, it's time to make an animatic. The purpose of the animatic is to work out the timing of each scene, and to roughly show how each scene transitions from one to the next. The animatic will also provide you with a more accurate idea of just how long your film will be. For convenience, you will want to number your audio clips in sequential order prior to import. This will allow you to import the audio clips as a batch and store them neatly in the Adobe Flash library.

8. *Background Design*
   Using the concept art you made during the visual development stage, along with your storyboards, you can decide how to design and draw your backgrounds. The first thing you may want to do is check your storyboards to see how often a background is being reused. Perhaps the only difference between two scenes taking place in the park is the distance of the camera from its subject. In this case, you can draw the scene as a wide shot and scale it up later for the close-up. The beauty of Adobe Flash is that once you've made your background into a symbol, it's saved in your library for repeated use, saving you the trouble of having to redraw it. When designing your background, composition and subtlety are key. You want your backgrounds to add to the story by including elements that establish a setting, create a mood, perhaps even foreshadow an event. A foggy harbor in the middle of the night will differ greatly from a department store during the holiday season. That said, try placing your characters in one of your new backgrounds and see if they can be seen clearly. It would be a shame to spend a great deal of time creating a lush, highly detailed background only to have it overpower your characters. Everything you create should be to aid in telling the story. If it's not, consider leaving it out.

9. *Animation*
   Animation can be approached several ways: pose to pose, straight ahead, or a combination of both. It's tempting to rely on Adobe Flash's motion tweening feature to do the animation, but as stated at the beginning of the book, Adobe Flash software is an authoring tool, not a crutch. As you've seen thus far, it takes a lot of work to get to this point. The animation stage is your time to really shine. Although your animatic will be entirely in one file, you will want to animate each scene in its own Adobe Flash file. Animation and audio can greatly increase the file's size, making it unmanageable. Keeping your animated scenes separate has two benefits. First, it reduces the risk of losing your entire project in the event of a computer crash. Second, there's a feeling of accomplishment when completing a scene and moving on to another one. Three months into a project, you'll come to appreciate small victories like that.

10. *Editing (Transitions, wipes)*
    Having completed the animation for every scene, the finish line is within sight, and you've earned a well-deserved pat on the back. After animating each scene in its own file, it's time to bring them all together in a video-

editing program, to add the transitions as indicated in your animatic, and to prepare your movie for export. As mentioned earlier, several programs can capably handle this task.

11. *Music and Sound Design*

When chosen correctly, music can add another layer of storytelling to your film. Imagine watching a horror movie with the sound turned down. How will you know when to be afraid? Picture the unsuspecting victim slowly walking down the creaky stairs into a cold, dark cellar. Can't you almost hear the intensity of the violins increase? What battle scene would be complete without the required banging of the timpani drums and other percussive instruments?

Sound effects serve the same purpose for moment-to-moment actions. What does the sound of a little bird tiptoeing across the floor sound like: the plucking of a violin or tapping of a xylophone perhaps? What about a tiptoeing overweight bear? Maybe a deeper bass or cello.

12. *Export and Delivery*

Knowing in advance where your story will be shown will determine its format (widescreen vs. 4:3 ratio), and its frame rate (Web vs. television). Many venues have strict guidelines for delivery, and you will want to approach your project with those in mind. You won't be able to reformat or change your frame rate after your project is done, so get these aspects solidified at the very beginning.

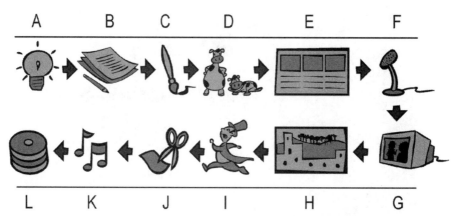

FIGURE 2-3   Diagram of the production pipeline (A. Idea, B. Script, C. Visual development, D. Model sheets, E. Storyboard, F. Voice record, G. Animatic, H. Background design, I. Animation, J. Editing, K. Sound design, L. Export/Delivery).

ORGANIZATION

With so many steps in the production process, it's easy to lose oneself unless there is a system in place. We will begin by creating a folder structure in which to maintain your assets and files. Figure 2-4 breaks down as follows: Your topmost folder will be named after your project/story/film. This folder will contain every file, asset, and resource pertaining to your film. Typically, a feature film is composed of three "acts" and a series of sequences within each act. Figure 2-4 shows a drop-down list of all the folders to be included in each Act. Thus, within the Act 1 folder, you will find the following subfolders: Audio, Backgrounds, Characters, Props, Reference, and a number of Sequence folders, abbreviated as "Seq_01, _02 . . ." A "sequence" contains all of the scenes taking place in one main location. For example, say a dramatic chase scene takes place in a busy train station. That sequence of events could include several cuts back and forth from the pursuer to the one being pursued, as well as shots of the station itself and the chaos taking place around the chase. All of those scenes can be placed within the train station sequence folder. As you can see in the example provided, Act 1/Seq_02/Sc_03 contains a work in progress (Scene 3) in its sixth version. Figure 2-5 shows the naming convention used for keeping these scenes in sequential order. The first few letters represent your project's title in abbreviated form followed by the second grouping, which contains the act number and sequence number as established in your storyboards. (This will be covered in detail in a later chapter.) The third group contains the scene

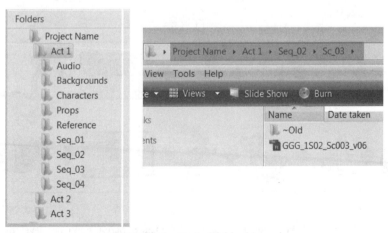

FIGURE 2-4   Typical folder hierarchy.

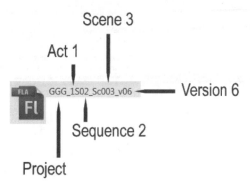

Scene 3

Act 1

GGG_1S02_Sc003_v06 ——— Version 6

Sequence 2

Project

FIGURE 2-5   File-naming convention. Save different versions as you progress. If a later version becomes corrupt, you still have an earlier version as a backup.

number, also indicated in your storyboards, concluding with the version number. Completing a scene can take anywhere from one day to several days, so always save multiple versions as you progress, just in case you decide to go back to an earlier version.

FILE PREPARATION

As mentioned earlier in this chapter, knowing in advance where your film will be shown factors into how you will make it. If its final destination is an .swf file on the Web, you will want to accommodate viewers with slower connections and animate your film at 15 frames per second (fps). The frame rate can be doubled to 30 fps if you upload it to the web as an .flv file, Quicktime® file, or to one of the many video-sharing Web sites out there. The nice thing about animating at 30 fps is that this frame rate allows you to burn the file to DVDs for viewing on your television and to submit it to film festivals. This leads to another very important point to consider: aspect ratio. Most televisions come with a 4:3 aspect ratio, but movie screens and newer high-definition (HD) televisions are set to a 16:9 aspect ratio. This means that newer screens are longer horizontally than they are tall. For now, 4:3 ratio is still the more common of the two, so setting your stage dimension to 720 pixels high by 540 pixels wide is a safe bet for viewing on TVs and film screens. For consistency, all examples in this book will be set to these dimensions. If you're targeting a mobile device, the Adobe Flash

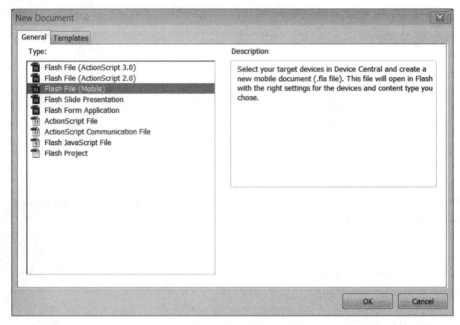

FIGURE 2-6   Accessing an Adobe® Flash® mobile template via File▶New.

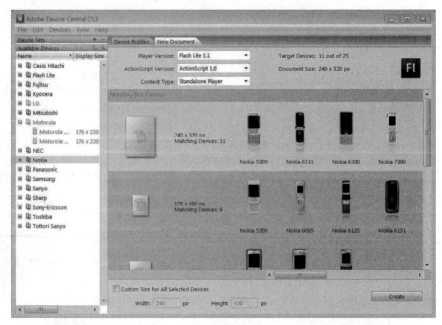

FIGURE 2-7   Adobe® Device Central® and its mobile device templates.

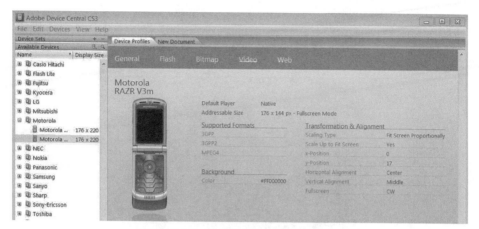

FIGURE 2-8   Mobile device detailed view.

platform offers an array of templates based on the specific phone or personal data assistant (PDA) via Adobe® Device Central®.

Let's prepare a new file by setting our frame rate and stage dimensions.

1. Open Adobe Flash and click the following: **File▶New▶Flash File▶OK**. Adobe Flash will open a new file with its default dimensions of 550 pixels × 400 pixels and a frame rate of 12 fps. These settings can easily be changed using the **Properties** panel located at the bottom of the screen.

FIGURE 2-9   Properties panel.

2. Click the **Size** button in the **Properties** panel. In the **Document Properties** panel, set your dimensions to 720 px wide by 540 px high. Enter **30** for the frame rate and either click **OK** to set just this file, or click the **Make Default** button to have Adobe Flash automatically open all new files with these settings. Then click **OK**.

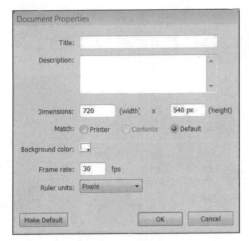

FIGURE 2-10   Document Properties panel.

YOUR WORKSPACE

Adobe Flash is an extremely powerful program. The simple fact that it is used by designers, programmers, and animators shows just what this software is capable of creating. The downside of this is that, with so many options, you may feel overwhelmed by all the panels available to you.

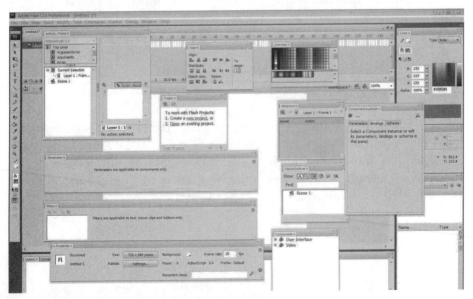

FIGURE 2-11   Some of Adobe® Flash®'s many panels.

Fortunately, you can customize your workspace to include only the panels you need to do your work efficiently. Let's do that now.

1. Open a new file.
2. Go to **Window▶Workspace▶Default**. This will give you a basic layout with which to begin your customization.
3. To add panels, click on **Window** from the top bar menu, and select the panels you need. Figure 2-12 highlights an animator's most often used set of panels.

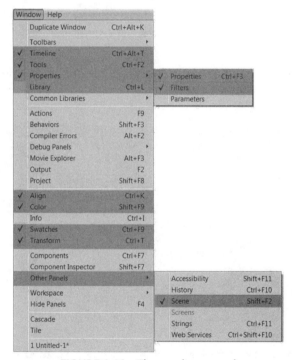

FIGURE 2-12   The panels you need.

4. To move the panels into place, simply click and drag the tabs into place. When the panel's border is highlighted in blue, let go. The panel will snap into place.

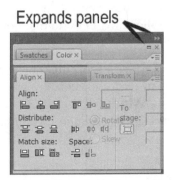

FIGURE 2-13   Drag panels from their tabs and snap them into place.

Figure 2-14 contains a sample layout with all of the panels most animators work with.

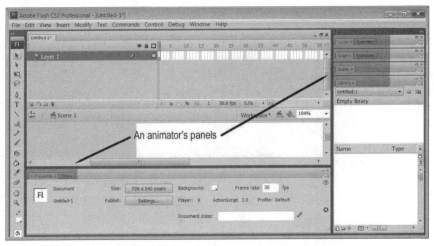

FIGURE 2-14   A typical animator's workspace.

5. Once you have all of your panels in their proper order, go to **Window▶ Workspace▶Save Current** and name your workspace. Click **OK**.

FIGURE 2-15   The **Save Workspace Layout** pop-up panel.

Your customized workspace is now saved and can always be accessed by going to **Window▶Workspace** and selecting your layout. If you need to delete a saved workspace, follow this path: **Window▶Workspace▶Manage**, and select the workspace you wish to delete. Close the window when you're done.

SUMMARY

In this chapter, we covered the hardware and software you'll need and the many steps involved in making an animated film using Adobe Flash. We detailed some methods for staying organized, and we have addressed some of the technical issues that all filmmakers must be aware of before beginning a project. Finally, we took a peek into Adobe Flash software by opening a new file and customizing our settings to fit our needs.

EXERCISES

Exercise 2.1

Create a list of all possible reference material for your project and begin gathering those items. This includes cutouts from magazines, typefaces, photographs of locations, video footage, your notebook sketches, sound files, etc.

Exercise 2.2

Using Figure 2-4 as your guide, customize a folder hierarchy for your project. Be sure to include a **Reference** folder for the assets gathered in Exercise 2.1.

Create subfolders as necessary to separate your .mp3s, .jpgs, .pngs, and any other files you plan to use. Refer to Figure 2-16 and Figure 2-17 for assistance.

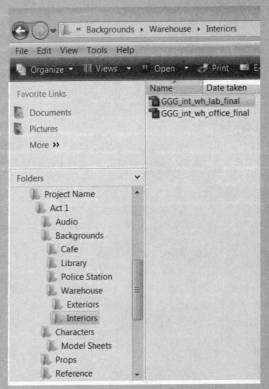

FIGURE 2-16   Folder structure showing files labeled as warehouse interiors.

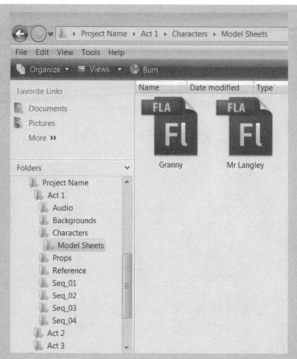

FIGURE 2-17   Folder structure showing character model sheets with their own files.

Chapter 3 GET THE LEAD OUT

"Nothing in life is to be feared; it is only to be understood."
—Marie Curie

APPLYING TRADITIONAL PRINCIPLES IN THE DIGITAL REALM

Though Adobe® Flash® is primarily a vector-based program, it does have the ability to import video and photography to incorporate into your film. The difference between an illustration you create directly in Adobe Flash and a photograph you've imported is its scalability. A photograph is made up of tiny colored squares known as pixels. As you can see in Figure 3-1, when a photo is enlarged, those squares start to blur. This is called pixellation and is not how you want viewers to see your film. The way to ensure that your images are the appropriate size upon import is to view them at 100% size on the stage. If, at 720 pixels wide × 540 pixels high, the image looks fine at 100%, then you should be good to go. The nice thing about drawing your artwork directly in Adobe Flash is that none of this applies. Vector art can be scaled infinitely without distortion. The same goes for art that was drawn using Adobe® Illustrator® software and imported into Adobe Flash.

SETTING YOUR PREFERENCES

Before beginning any project, it's important to set your preferences. For now, we will focus on a feature you will probably use the most: **Undo**.

Original vector

Original raster

Vector enlarged   Photo enlarged

FIGURE 3-1   A vector image compared to a photograph, also known as a raster image.

1. Launch Adobe Flash.
2. From the top menu bar, click **Edit ▶Preferences**.

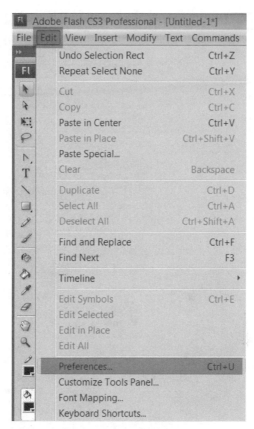

FIGURE 3-2   Edit ▶Preferences.

3. Choose the **General** category and click the **Undo** drop-down menu. Select
    Object-level Undo. Input **100** for the number of levels. Click **OK**.

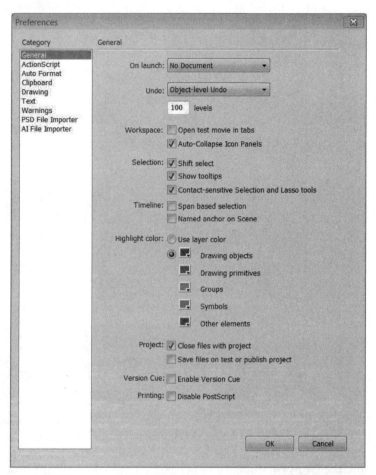

FIGURE 3-3   The **Preferences** panel within Adobe® Flash®.

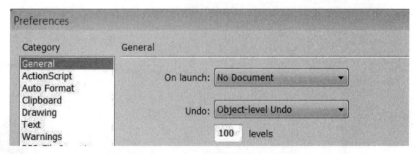

FIGURE 3-4   Set up your **Undo** levels right from the start.

KEYBOARD SHORTCUTS

Drawing and animating requires a great deal of repetition. To maintain a flow during the creative process, it's important to learn your keyboard shortcuts. As with all programs, Adobe Flash has a list of preexisting shortcuts that can easily be seen by hovering over any tool.

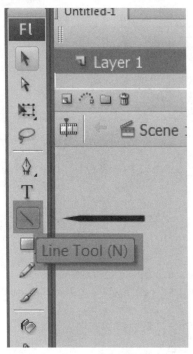

FIGURE 3-5   Hover over any tool to see its label and keyboard shortcut in parentheses.

Here is a list of the keyboard shortcuts you will add to an existing set in order to create your own customized set.

Convert Lines to Fills	Ctrl+Alt+'
Flip Horizontal	/
Flip Vertical	'
Snap to Objects tool	Ctrl+'

Let's customize our shortcuts now.

1. Open the Adobe Flash application and go to **Edit ►Keyboard Shortcuts** from the top menu bar.
2. Click the **Duplicate Set** icon and type a name in the text field box. Click **OK**.

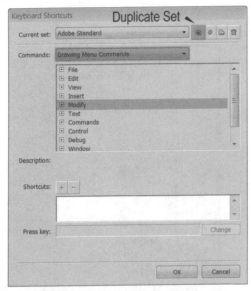

FIGURE 3-6   **Keyboard Shortcuts** panel.

FIGURE 3-7   Type a name in the **Duplicate** pop-up panel.

3. You'll notice that the new set you just created is now listed as the **Current set** at the top of the panel. Choose **Drawing Menu Commands** from the **Commands** drop-down list. Click the **+** symbol next to the word **Modify**. Scroll down to **Shape** and click it to reveal the **Convert Lines to Fills** command.

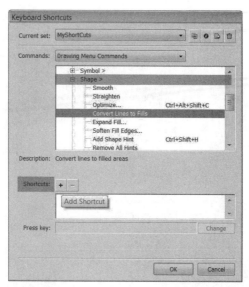

FIGURE 3-8 Adding a **Convert Lines to Fills** keyboard shortcut.

4. Add a shortcut by clicking the **+** symbol next to the **Shortcuts** heading (See Figure 3-8).

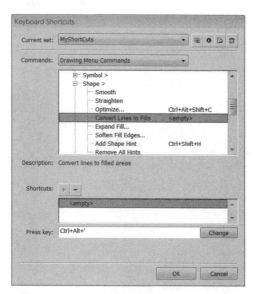

FIGURE 3-9 Current keyboard shortcut is empty.

5. In the **Press Key** text field, type in the shortcut **Ctrl+Alt+'** (See Figure 3-10).

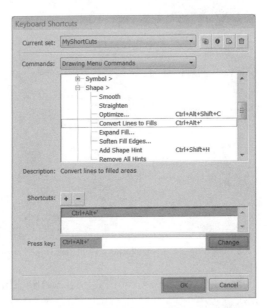

FIGURE 3-10   Entering your shortcut keys.

6. Once the change has been made, click the **Change** button to submit your shortcut. Follow the same steps to complete the other three shortcuts listed above, and click **OK** to finish.

Note: Flip Horizontal and **Vertical** are located under **Modify/Transform**, and **Snap to Objects** is located under **View/Snapping**. All three are listed under **Drawing Menu Commands**.

PROGRAM INTERFACE

If you are already familiar with other Adobe® programs, the Adobe Flash interface should seem somewhat familiar. The biggest difference is the timeline and the stage. The timeline is made up of a series of numbers beginning with the number one. The moment you draw or import something onto the blank stage, Adobe Flash adds a tiny black dot on the timeline. That dot is called a keyframe. We will cover how keyframes work in Chapter 7 when we discuss animation.

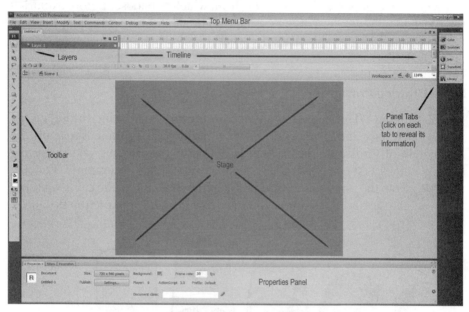

FIGURE 3-11   User interface.

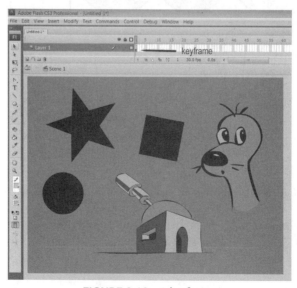

FIGURE 3-12   A keyframe.

DRAWING

Flash offers a number of drawing tools from which to choose. Before exploring the tool bar, however, let's discuss some traditional drawing principles that will improve your drawing skills no matter what your drawing surface: paper, canvas, or digital tablet.

Some Drawing Principles

Foreshortening—The biggest challenge in drawing is breaking through a flat drawing surface and giving your drawings depth. One solution is to apply the principle of foreshortening, which is defined as shortening and distorting parallel lines as they go into space. Take a can of soup, for example. Looking directly from the top, you see a circle, but as the can is tilted, the circle squashes into an ellipse, and the sides become narrower as they go into the distance.

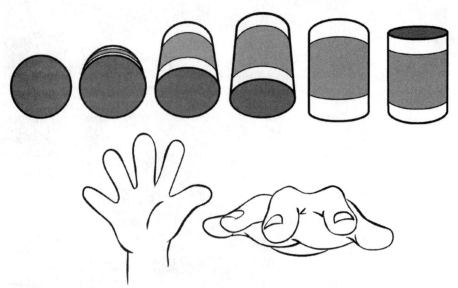

FIGURE 3-13   Foreshortening illustrated with a can of soup and a hand.

Overlap—Placing one object in front of another is also an effective way to create depth. No matter how simple your drawings may be, applying overlap instantly adds depth.

FIGURE 3-14   Overlapping simple shapes and some flowers.

Contour—If you want to add volume to your drawings, try "describing" the shape by adding simple lines that follow your shape's contour. As your skills progress, you will be able to apply shading to achieve the same effect.

FIGURE 3-15   Contour applied to form a tree.

Size—Drawing one object bigger than another creates the illusion that the bigger object is closer to you. Use this principle in combination with the others to truly have your drawings jump off the page.

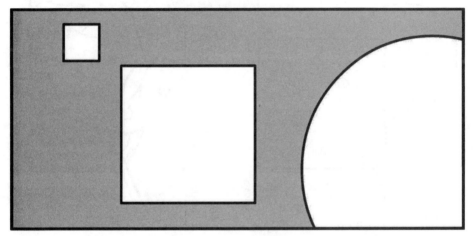

FIGURE 3-16   The principle of size used with simple shapes.

Silhouette—Though this principle is most applied when posing your characters, it's a good concept to keep in mind when deciding on an angle for your drawing. Opening up your subject's silhouette helps clarify your subject's intention.

FIGURE 3-17   Choose an interesting angle, and show it in silhouette form to clarify your drawing. Compare different angles of an airplane.

Shading—By adding a light source, shading helps add volume to your drawing. The farther something is from the light source, the darker it gets. To further enhance the form, add a bit of reflected light bouncing off the surface on which your object is standing. (See Figure 3-18.)

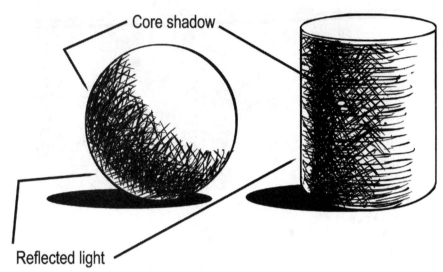

FIGURE 3-18   Shading a sphere and cylinder with one light source in mind.

Perspective—In essence, all of the principles mentioned above apply rules of perspective. The definition of perspective, for our purpose, can be boiled down to the relationship of one object to another on a two-dimensional plane. Perspective is most noticeable when drawing groups of things. Notice the illustration in Figure 3-19. The illusion of depth is created by illustrating objects on three planes: foreground, middle ground, and background. When drawing landscapes, keep these three planes in mind, and the worlds you create will be ones people will want to dive into.

FIGURE 3-19 Sketched directly in Adobe® Flash® with the brush tool, this illustration uses all of the drawing principles.

DRAWING IN ADOBE FLASH

Now that we have some drawing principles under our belt, we can begin applying them directly in Adobe Flash. There are six tools that we'll be using most to create our characters and backgrounds. Hover over each tool to begin learning its shortcut. Memorizing these and the four you added earlier will save you valuable time. Using Figure 3-20 as a guide, the shortcuts, from top to bottom are as follows: Select (**v**), Subselect (**a**), Line (**n**), Oval (**o**), or Rectangle (**r**), Pencil (**y**), Brush (**b**), Ink Bottle (**s**), and Paint Bucket (**k**).

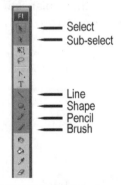

FIGURE 3-20 Drawing tools.

Let's begin by drawing some simple lines using the **Line** and **Pencil** tools.

1. Tap **n** on your keyboard to select the **Line** tool and draw a line.
2. Tap **v** on your keyboard to select the **Selection** tool.
3. Hover over the endpoint of the line and notice the small icon that appears next to your cursor. Grab that endpoint and pull the line stretching the line in and out.

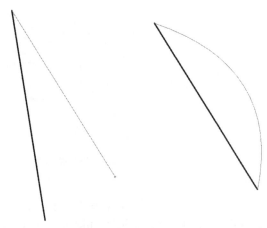

FIGURE 3-21   Adjust your line by pushing, pulling, or bending it.

4. Hover over the middle of the line, and notice that the small icon has changed into a curve. Pull the line from the center, and notice how it curves the line.

TIP

Hold down the **Ctrl** key on your keyboard as you pull from the center of your line and you'll see that Adobe Flash has added a new point to your line.

---

5. Click on the keyframe in Frame 1, and press **Delete** on your keyboard to clear your stage.
6. Tap **y** on your keyboard to select the **Pencil** tool, and draw a squiggle that has intersecting lines.

7. Click anywhere on the squiggle to select it. Move your selection elsewhere on the stage. Notice how Adobe Flash treats lines that intersect as segments.

FIGURE 3-22   Intersecting lines are treated as segments and can be manipulated individually.

8. Clear the stage, and draw two more lines that do not touch. Find the icon at the bottom of the tool bar that looks like a magnet, and use your new shortcut for snapping to objects (**Ctrl+'**). With the magnet tool selected, tap **v** on your keyboard to select the **Selection** tool, and pull one of the endpoints toward the other. Flash lets you know that the two endpoints are connected by displaying a dark circle over their union. Release the point to connect the lines.

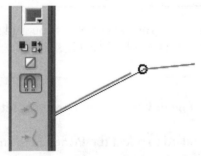

FIGURE 3-23   Snap two endpoints together by selecting the **Magnet** tool.

The **Subselection** tool allows you to further refine curves by providing handles that you can push, pull, and rotate.

1. Use the **Pencil** tool to draw a simple "S" curve.
2. Tap **a** on your keyboard to select the **Subselection** tool, and drag across your stage to select the curve. The Adobe Flash program shows you various handles to choose from. Grab one and move it around to manipulate your shape.

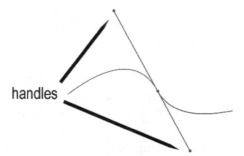

FIGURE 3-24   The **Subselection** tool's handles.

Both the **Line** tool and the **Pencil** tool offer an array of choices when it comes to line quality. To view those options, draw a few lines and click one with the **Selection** tool (**v**). The **Properties** panel now gives you the option to change the color of the stroke, change its thickness, choose a different type of line, and customize the quality of the stroke.

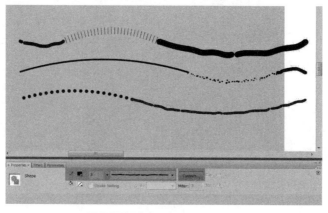

FIGURE 3-25   Line properties.

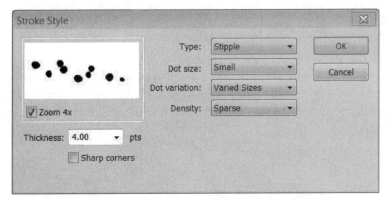

FIGURE 3-26   Customizing your line quality via the **Stroke Style** pop-up panel.

The **Pencil** tool acts somewhat like a real pencil except that you can give Adobe Flash some control over your line. Looking at the bottom of Figure 3-27, you can see that there are three pencil modes: **Straighten**, **Smooth**, and **Ink**. Draw a few lines in the different modes to see the differences. They may be slight, but when used in combination with the line properties in Figures 3-25 and 3-26, they could be enough to give you the line quality you're looking for.

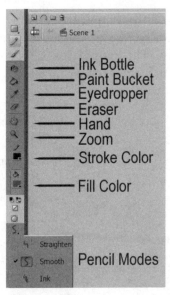

FIGURE 3-27   Additional tools.

The **Shape** tools you will find most useful are the **Oval** tool and the **Rectangle** tool. Let's draw some shapes and see how we can manipulate them.

1. On a clear stage, draw a square with the rectangle tool.

> **TIP**
>
> By holding the **Shift** key while dragging, you will attain a perfect square. If you hold **Shift+Alt**, your square will draw out from its center point.

2. Double-click inside the square to select it, and move it to another part of the stage. Deselect it, and draw a perfect circle next to the square.
3. Click once inside the square, and move your selection to a clear part of the stage. Notice that it only grabbed the "fill" and not the "stroke."

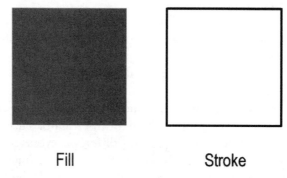

Fill   Stroke

FIGURE 3-28   Shapes are made up of fills and strokes. Their properties can be changed separately.

4. Select the fill, and change its color by clicking the **Fill Color** palette in the toolbar. Do the same with the stroke by double-clicking it and choosing another color from the **Stroke Color** palette in the tool bar.

Note: Remember, clicking twice selects the entire square. Clicking once only selects a segment because the lines are intersecting.

5. Let's add a stroke back onto the square. Choose the **Ink Bottle** tool from the tool bar, and click inside the square's fill. Voila! The stroke is back. To fill the empty square, choose the **Paint Bucket** tool from the tool bar, and click inside the square.

6. Use the **Selection** tool to reshape the square by pulling its corners and bending its sides.

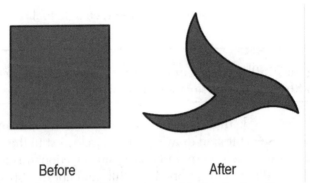

Before   After

FIGURE 3-29   Transform a square into an abstract bird by simply pulling corners and bending sides with the **Selection** tool.

7. Clear the stage, and draw a circle and square. Give each shape a different color fill and stroke.
8. Double-click the circle and partially cover the square with it. Click elsewhere on the stage to deselect it.
9. Double-click the circle again, and move it away from the square. It looks like the hungry circle bit off a chunk of the square. This can be avoided in a few ways: by drawing objects on different layers, by grouping your objects as you draw them, or by converting your drawings to symbols. All three techniques will be covered in detail when we begin drawing our characters and backgrounds.

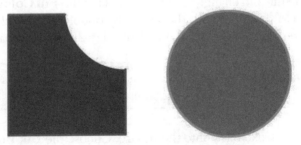

FIGURE 3-30   Overlapping objects temporarily on one layer can cause you to lose some parts of your drawing.

The **Eyedropper** tool works like you'd expect; it can be used to "soak up" the color of both strokes and fills. After soaking up a color, Adobe Flash conveniently changes the tool into either an ink bottle or a paint bucket, so you can drop it onto another shape. Let's explore the **Paint Bucket** and its different modes.

1. Draw a circle and remove the fill, leaving only the stroke.
2. With your **Selection** tool, select a tiny portion of the circle's stroke by dragging across it. Delete that portion, leaving a small gap in your circle.

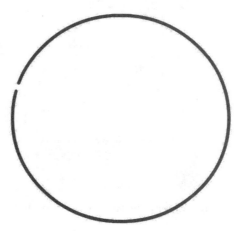

FIGURE 3-31 Circle with a gap.

3. Try filling the circle with a fill color. Depending on the size of your gap, the Adobe Flash program may or may not fill it. This calls for one of Adobe Flash's four gap modes. Try filling in the circle with the different modes. Chances are, the **Close Large Gaps** mode will be the one that works. Of the four, this is the mode you are most likely to rely on when rendering your drawings. Of course, if the gap is too large, then you're better off to simply close it.

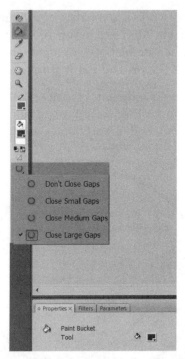

FIGURE 3-32   Closing the gap with the **Paint Bucket** tool.

Earlier, we covered three **Pencil** modes available to you before you begin sketching. But what if your finished sketch is too rough, and you want to smooth it out a bit? Let's do a simple exercise to see what your options are.

1. Draw a quick sketch using the **Pencil** tool in **Ink** mode to keep it squiggly.
2. Use the **Selection** tool to select the entire drawing, and click the **Smooth** icon in the toolbar a few times. As you do, watch how your drawing changes shape.
3. Go back to the original sketch by tapping **Ctrl+z** a few times.
4. Now select the sketch again and try the **Straighten** mode.

While the results are relatively unpredictable, it's common practice to quickly sketch out an idea or pose, smooth it out with the **Smooth** tool, and then clean up your drawing further by pushing, pulling, and bending lines as we learned earlier in this chapter.

Original Sketch   Smooth Mode applied   Straighten Mode applied

FIGURE 3-33   **Smooth** mode vs. **Straighten** mode on an existing sketch.

If you're looking for a way to draw that feels more like sketching with a pencil on paper, then the **Brush** tool is your answer. With the option of adjusting brush shape, brush size, and pressure sensitivity, you can quickly get your idea down without losing the character of your drawing.

FIGURE 3-34   A quick sketch using the **Brush** tool with pressure sensitivity to establish gesture and pose.

Another thing to know about the **Brush** tool is that it is a fill, so it can be reshaped by pushing and pulling its sides and handles.

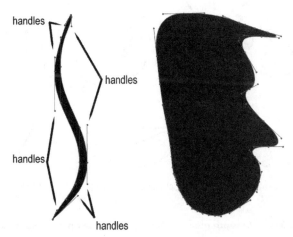

FIGURE 3-35   A brush stroke before and after pulling its sides.

If you're more comfortable sketching with the **Pencil** tool, but prefer that your final drawing have some variety in line thickness, you're in luck. By selecting your line work and then going to **Modify ▶ Shape ▶ Convert Lines to Fills**, you can change the way your lines behave, and you can alter them the same way you would any other shape.

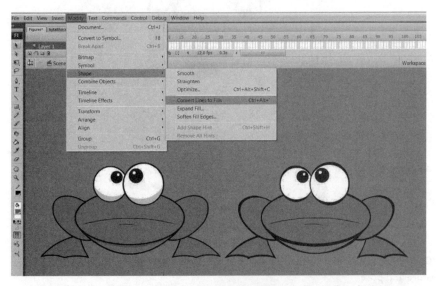

FIGURE 3-36   **Convert Lines to Fills** for creating a variety in line thickness.

Let's take a look at a couple of other things you can do with fills.

1. In a new file, draw an ellipse with no stroke.
2. Select the ellipse and go to **Modify ►Shape ►Expand Fill**.

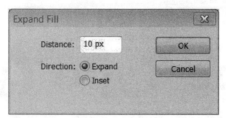

FIGURE 3-37   **Expand Fill** pop-up panel.

3. In the **Expand Fill** pop-up panel, choose **Expand** and type **10 px** in the **Distance** text field box. You have now expanded the size of your fill by 10 pixels. Choosing **Inset** will shrink it by that amount.
4. Clear the stage and draw another ellipse.
5. Select the ellipse and go to **Modify ►Shape ►Soften Fill Edges**.

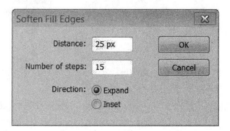

FIGURE 3-38   **Soften Fill Edges** pop-up panel.

6. In the **Soften Fill Edges** pop-up panel, type **25 px** in the **Distance** text field box and **15** for the number of steps. Again, choose **Expand**. Zoom in if necessary, and you will see that Adobe Flash has softened the outer edge of your shape. This can be one of many ways to create a ground shadow.

If your library of fonts is limited, there is a way to take an existing font and alter it for your use. Unfortunately, you won't be able to save it as a font, so this technique is primarily for a header or title, not for body copy. But it's nice to know that you have this ability. Let's try it.

1. Pick a simple font, and type a word.

2. Use the shortcut **Ctrl+B** to break it apart. In the top menu bar, it is accessible via **Modify ▶Break Apart**. At this point, each letter is grouped individually and can be moved around.
3. Break it apart again. The text is now raw art, just like any other shape made with a fill.

FIGURE 3-39   The three stages of breaking apart text.

4. Push and pull the sides of each letter, and arrange them as you please.
5. You now have your very own title.

FIGURE 3-40   Breaking apart text for customization.

Like most programs, Adobe Flash comes with an **Eraser** tool, but you may find it easier just to select the items you want to delete and tap the **Delete** key on your keyboard. This saves time from switching tools back and forth. In any case, some nifty features are worth exploring. Look at Figure 3-41 to see the eraser's five modes.

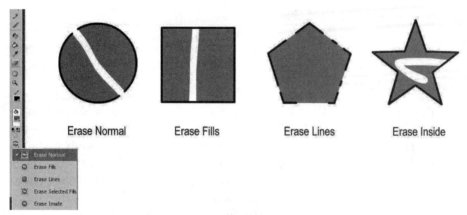

FIGURE 3-41   The **Eraser** tool and its various modes.

The **Zoom** tool works like any other application. Its shortcut to zoom in is **Ctrl+** (plus key), and to zoom out press **Ctrl-** (minus key).

The **Hand** tool is used to move around the stage.

> **TIP**
>
> A faster method is to hold down the space bar and move around with either your mouse or stylus.

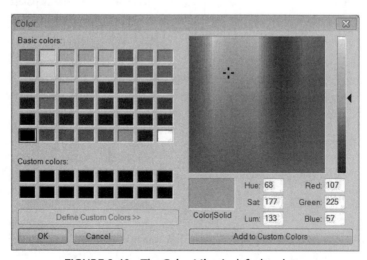

FIGURE 3-42   The **Color Mixer's** default palette.

WORKING WITH COLOR

Eventually, you will want to establish a color palette for your film, to suggest mood, time of day, genre, or time period. This means customizing your color palette. Let's do a trial run now.

1. Launch Adobe Flash and start a new file. Go to **Window ▶ Workspace ▶Default**. This places all of your windows in order. If you ever find that you are missing a palette, you can always grab it via the **Window** drop-down menu and add it to your existing layout.
2. Click the drop-down menu from the **Swatches** palette, and click **Clear Colors** to start out with a clean color palette. You'll see that the Adobe Flash program starts you off with two swatches, black and white.

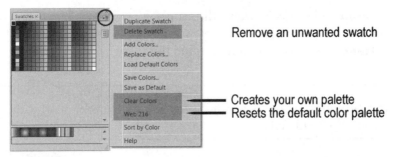

FIGURE 3-43   To customize your colors, begin with the **Swatches** palette.

3. Pick a color from the spectrum in the **Color** palette.

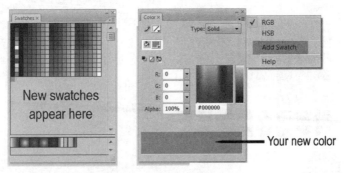

FIGURE 3-44   Choose a color from the spectrum, and add your new swatch via the **Color** palette.

4. Open its drop-down menu, and choose **Add Swatch**. Your new swatch will appear in the **Swatches** palette.

5. Add a few more swatches and choose **Save Colors** from the **Swatches** palette drop-down menu.

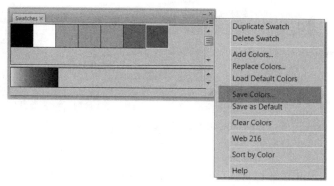

FIGURE 3-45   Save your customized palette for future use.

6. Give your new color palette a descriptive name, and click **Save**.

FIGURE 3-46   Naming your new set and saving it as its own .clr file.

7. If you click the **Fill Color** icon in the toolbar, you'll see that your new palette has replaced the old one. Whenever you want to return to the default palette, simply choose **Web 216** from the **Swatches** palette. Go ahead and do that now.

GRADIENTS

Both lines and fills can have either linear or radial gradients applied to them from the **Color** palette. To add more colors, simply click just below the thin spectrum. To adjust how the gradient appears on the shape, you can slide the "**little house**" icons left or right.

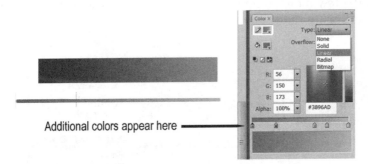

Additional colors appear here

FIGURE 3-47   Gradients.

Another way to further refine a gradient's appearance inside is to use the **Gradient Transform** tool. Once you have chosen your colors and filled your shape with a gradient, select the **Gradient Transform** tool from the tool bar, click your shape, and move, stretch, scale, and rotate its handles to attain the effect you're looking for.

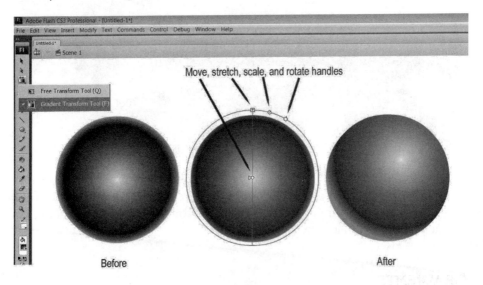

FIGURE 3-48   The **Gradient Transform** tool.

Often, gradients are not used very effectively. It is tempting to quickly apply a two-color gradient onto a shape and be done with it. Unfortunately, the end result does not look very professional. The key to an effective gradient is subtlety. A file named **gradient.fla** has been provided in the enclosed DVD for your exploration. It contains some examples of three-dimensional objects made with gradients and the other tools discussed in this chapter.

ADVANCED SHAPES

Some shapes are more quickly drawn with preexisting tools than from scratch. Primarily, they are polygons, rectangles with rounded corners, and multipointed stars. This is how to go about making such shapes.

1. To draw a rectangle with rounded corners, select the **Rectangle** icon from the tool bar and maximize the **Properties** panel. Adjust the amount of the roundness by moving the slider up to **35**, and then drawing the shape.

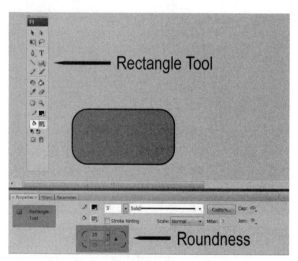

FIGURE 3-49   Adjusting the roundness of a rectangle in the **Properties** panel.

2. To draw a polygon, click and hold down the **Rectangle** tool, and select the **PolyStar** tool at the bottom of the list. Maximize the **Properties** panel, and click on the **Options** button. Under **Style**, choose **polygon** and type in **8** for the **Number of Sides**. Leave the **Star point size** as is. Click **OK**. Drag your cursor across the stage to draw the shape.

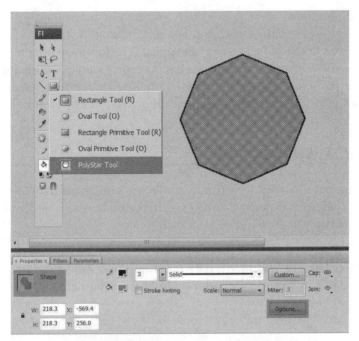

FIGURE 3-50   **PolyStar Properties** panel.

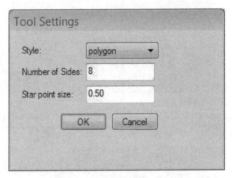

FIGURE 3-51   **Tool Settings** pop-up panel.

3. To draw a star, follow the same procedure as in Step 2, but choose **Star** under **Style**, and type in a different number for **Number of Sides**. Play with different settings to create various shapes.

LAYERING

As our drawings become more sophisticated, we will want to add and name new layers. Layering will also be crucial during the animation stage. Here's a simple exercise for creating and naming new layers.

1. Open a new file. Create two new layers by clicking the **Insert Layer** icon twice.
2. To name a layer, double-click its current name. In our case, it will most likely be "**Layer 1**," "**Layer 2**," and "**Layer 3**." Name the top layer "**Top**," the middle layer "**Middle**," and the bottom layer "**Bottom**."
3. Now rearrange the layer order by clicking once on any layer and dragging it up or down to move it. Do this a few times just to get the hang of it.
4. To delete a layer, select the layer you wish to delete and click the **Delete Layer** icon (tiny trash can).

TIP

You can also delete a layer by selecting the layer, right-clicking your mouse, and choosing **Delete Layer** from the drop-down menu. You'll find that many actions that have shortcuts can also be accomplished by right-clicking your mouse. If you change your mind and want that layer back, press **Ctrl-z** to undo, and the layer will return.

FIGURE 3-52   The **Insert Layer** and **Delete Layer** icons and the right-click submenu.

IMPORTING A BITMAP

As mentioned at the beginning of this chapter, it is possible to import photographs into your Adobe Flash file and to treat them as you would any other graphic. Let's see what we can do to a photographic image.

1. Go to **File ▶Import ▶Import to Stage**. Choose the image you would like to import. Your image now exists in three places: your stage, your **Library**, and your color palette. Your **Library** should be on the right-hand side of your workspace. If it is not expanded, double-click its tab. If your **Library** is missing, go to **Window ▶Library** to retrieve it. We will explore the **Library** in depth in a future chapter. For now, it's good to know that the **Library** stores items that can be used repeatedly without increasing the file's size. Simply drag the item out of the **Library** and onto your stage, and a duplicate will appear. Do this as often as you like.

FIGURE 3-53　Imported bitmap in the **Library**.

2. Now open your **Color** palette. From the **Type** drop-down menu, scroll down to **Bitmap**, and you'll see your newly imported image.

FIGURE 3-54   Imported bitmap in the **Color** palette.

3. Draw an ellipse or circle, and you'll see your photograph inside. This means that your photograph can be pulled and trimmed just like any other fill.

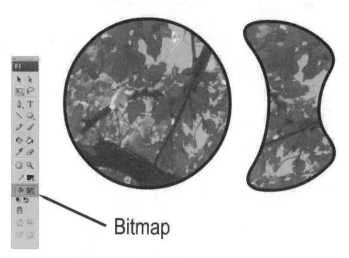

FIGURE 3-55   A bitmap acting as a fill.

TRANSFORM TOOLS

The **Transform** tool on your tool bar (shortcut: **Q**) can do more than scale and rotate. It can skew, distort, and reshape individual points, and it can offer some perspective. Figures 3-56 and 3-57 show the various **Transform** tools and how they can be applied.

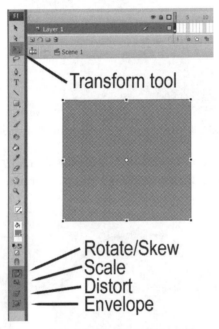

FIGURE 3-56 The **Transform** tools.

FIGURE 3-57   Some shapes made with the **Distort** and **Envelope** tools.

In addition to a shape's sides, its center point can also be adjusted to control its rotation. To move the center point, select and drag it to another area anywhere on the stage. It can be within the shape or even outside it. Then hover over the shape's corner and rotate it.

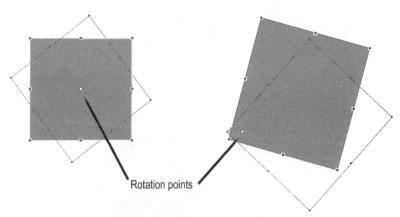

Rotation points

FIGURE 3-58   Editing a shape's rotation point.

SUMMARY

In this chapter, we learned how to customize our preferences, how to utilize keyboard shortcuts, and how to navigate the interface. Some traditional drawing principles were introduced to improve our drawing skills, and their application in Adobe Flash to achieve the "look" we want for our film was also discussed. Finally, we customized our own color palettes, applied gradients to shapes for a three-dimensional effect, and explored the various options offered within the **Transform** tool in the tool bar.

EXERCISES

Exercise 3.1

Open **gradient.fla** in the enclosed DVD, and try recreating its objects in a separate file. Be sure to name your layers. To see exactly how the gradients were made, click the gradient itself, and the color combination will appear in the **Color** panel. The same can be done for the highlights that were manipulated with the **Gradient Transform** tool.

Exercise 3.2

Refer to the various perspective diagrams in Figure 3-59 below to help you visualize what your world will look like as you continue to develop your story. Lay some tracing paper over each diagram and quickly sketch out a cityscape and a landscape in thumbnail form. Try not to get bogged down with details. The idea is simply to create a sense of depth. Feel free to use photographic reference, or better yet, find someplace outside and sketch on location.

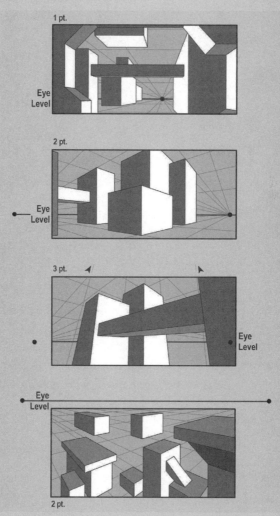

FIGURE 3-59   Different angles of perspective.

Chapter **4** THE WRITE STUFF

"People have forgotten how to tell a story. Stories don't have a middle or an end anymore. They usually have a beginning that never stops beginning."

—Steven Spielberg

BRAINSTORMING A CONCEPT

Stories serve different purposes. Some stories are meant to entertain or educate. Others are meant to persuade. As a storyteller, it is your goal to engage the viewer, pull the audience in, and not let them go until the very last frame of your film. Perhaps your intent is to sell a product to a specific consumer, to teach the alphabet to school kids, to present your company's third-quarter performance to its board of directors, to explain how gravity works, or to convince people to care about your charity. Regardless of what you hope your story will accomplish, it all begins with the story's concept. Let's examine some ways to approach a few of the examples given above.

Using a Story to Promote

Imagine that your task is to make an animated short that persuades people to buy a watch. Some questions you may ask yourself are these: What type of watch is it? An old timepiece like a pocket watch? A sports watch that can be worn hundreds of feet below water? A vanity watch for young executives on the go? The answers to these questions will open up countless concepts for your story. If the watch harkens back to a time long past, then you may want to begin by establishing your story's setting. Is it during the Renaissance? The Victorian era? Times like these are loaded with potential because of their rich history and vibrant cultures.

If your watch is for divers, then perhaps a more dramatic sequence showing the value of time to a diver could be your approach. Imagine being deep beneath the sea with only a limited amount of oxygen left in your tank. Knowing how much time you have left can be a matter of life and death. Having a watch that can withstand the pressure can make the difference.

If your product caters to young executives on the go, think of situations where time is of the essence, such as catching a plane for an overseas business trip or racing to an important business meeting. You might try approaching your subject from different angles like humor, drama, and suspense.

Using Your Story to Teach

Teachers are always coming up with innovative ways to convey information to their students, and for good reason. Today's kids are bombarded with information from television, radio, cell phones, video games, magazines, the Internet, and more. Rather than compete with all these media, many educators have decided to embrace them and to use them to their advantage. Interactive books and games have emerged that are designed to teach multiple subjects. Something as simple as the alphabet could be turned into a story by using each initial to represent a character or element in the story. Let's try it and see what happens: An "A"irplane flown by a "B"rown bear and striped "C"at was heading to "D"enver in "E"arly "F"ebruary. A "G"iant "H"ailstorm was reported to hit just as they were scheduled to arrive. To prevent "I"njury, the local fire department poured five thousand pounds of "J"ello and "K"elp onto the tarmac to cushion their "L"anding. Just beyond the "M"ountains, visibility was reduced to "N"othing, and the pilot "O"rdered the "P"assengers to be "Q"uiet and "R"emain in their "S"eats. "T"urbulence from the storm clouds "U"nder the belly of the plane shook it "V"iolently from side to side for "W"hat seemed like an eternity until . . .

This story is far from complete, but remember, we are still in the brainstorming stage. The purpose of this exercise is simply to plant a seed and see what grows. This particular example reveals some challenges that may be worth pursuing. One challenge might be to use words that are at the students' grade level. Another might be to make the subject matter relevant to something they're learning in their studies, be it science, art, music, or history. This could help the teacher make cross-reference among lessons. Now imagine combining this story with imagery and animation. By the twenty-sixth letter you could have a richly textured and complex tale.

Using Your Story to Present

The beauty of "story" is that anything can be presented in an interesting manner, no matter how mundane the subject matter. The explanation of how we went from sitting on the classroom floor captivated by our teacher's storytelling to staring blankly at circular graphs and bar charts in our adulthood is enough to keep psychologists busy for a lifetime. Turning those sleep-inducing charts into dynamic presentations, however, is where we come in. Take a company's third-quarter performance as an example. Let's pretend that the company grows bananas and exports them to stores worldwide. Sales were down early in the quarter but are on a steady rise. Your task is to present this dry information in a lighthearted, memorable way, with a hint of hope at the end.

For starters, we'll need an attention-grabbing character to take us along for the ride. Since the company grows bananas, a monkey will do. How you show the company's profits and losses can vary. One option could be to show the monkey stealing bananas from the plants and running off with them (losses). Each time he eats one, he throws the peel over his shoulder, "planting" a metaphorical seed in the ground, thus sprouting a new bushel of bananas (profits) for later in the season. Not a bad idea, but this too, is far from a story. As you'll read in the next section, there are a few ingredients we still need to apply in order for these concepts to blossom into riveting stories.

As you continue to think about a concept, you may decide that the initial idea doesn't work. That's okay. A writer's first idea is rarely the one that the viewer sees in the end. What's important is that you continue to search for creative ways to disseminate your information. Scribble as many ideas as you can, and choose the one that you connect with the most. If it strikes a chord with you, then it will strike an emotional chord with your viewer as well. Look for ways to incorporate familiar situations into your story. Some examples of things we can all relate to are these: losing something you care about, fear of the unknown, the joy of attaining a goal, the anxiety of facing a seemingly difficult challenge, the longing for something someone else already possesses, or the excitement of starting something new. Every one of these concepts can be applied to anything from selling a loaf of bread to explaining a difficult scientific principle. Once you've laid this foundation, you can begin building your story.

ELEMENTS OF A STORY

Going from concept to script can be approached a number of ways. Some writers begin by defining their characters; others establish a plot. Let's take a look at their differences.

Characters

In Chapter 1, we touched on the importance of developing your characters by getting to know what makes them tick. How we respond to situations, or approach other people, has just as much to do with where we come from as it does our current surroundings. Your characters should be no different. To understand your characters' motivations, you will want to write a brief biography for each of them. Some things you will want to explore include your characters' age, gender, family members, childhood, education, quirks, likes and dislikes, dreams, strengths and weaknesses, life lessons, unusual encounters, life-altering moments, surroundings growing up, etc. The more you get to know your characters at this stage, the easier it will be to decide how they will act in a given situation.

Below is an example of a biography written for a story about a retired marine turned crime-fighting superhero, who also happens to be an elderly grandmother living in a suburban retirement home.

The Biography of Granny Goodguns

The youngest of seven siblings, Katherine Goodhue was born and raised in Dublin, Ireland, with six brothers and a cat named Mr. Whiskers. At the age of ten, Katherine was witness to a turbulent time where many were killed in action, fighting for their beliefs and country. Her father, a former soldier, was one of them. To protect her child from harm, Katherine's mother reluctantly, but hopefully, hid her daughter on a cargo ship headed west.

Arriving in New York, cold and alone, Katherine had nowhere to turn for survival but her own instincts. This included stealing fruit from open-air markets and sleeping in subways to keep warm. "Be strong like your father," her mother told her on deck just before giving her a final embrace and good-bye kiss. When things got rough, young Katherine would remember her family and reminisce about the times she would dress up Mr. Whiskers in fancy pajamas and confide in him while drinking tea.

After several arrests for shoplifting, Katherine was sent to a juvenile hall at the age of 12. Constantly teased for talking to her "invisible cat," Katherine quietly vowed to avenge herself by "punishing bullies like that when I leave this place." Over time, Katherine's resourcefulness and sincere efforts to mature were recognized by the resident psychologist. Sympathizing with Katherine's past, the psychologist adopted her and raised her as her own. Although she was then raised in a loving home, Katherine's past was never far behind, so at the age of 18, she enlisted with the U.S. Marines, where she excelled and proved herself to be worthy of the Special Forces. To the dismay of the local police force and the amusement of the press, Katherine, finally retired, used her decades of military experience to continue serving her country by secretly "cleaning up the decay in today's society." These acts of vigilantism, combined with her calling card (a burnt hair curler), caused her to be dubbed Granny Goodguns.

FIGURE 4-1   Creating a character's world.

A brief biography like the one written above will provide you with an insight into your characters' personalities and help you understand who these people are and how they became that way. Once you have assembled your characters' biographies, you can start thinking of how your characters relate to the story's initial concept. What is it that your main character wants? What drives him/her to pursue that goal? Who or what stands in his/her way? How is your character affected by the pursuit of that goal? Does your character ever reach it? Explain your answer. Sometimes getting what we want isn't all it was advertised to be. Is your character worse off for reaching that goal? The answers to all these questions can be answered in any format you like: typed page by page, written on Post-it notes, or drawn as diagrams. Choose what's most comfortable for you. Since you are still in the exploration stage, it is recommended that you remain flexible with your assumptions; the introduction of plot could spin your story in a whole new direction.

Plot

Also known as a storyline, plot is defined as a series of events or actions that make up a story. Regardless of its length, the series of events typically takes place in this order:

1. Exposition—The beginning of the story, used to introduce characters and set up the story. The goal is to create excitement in your audience, pull them in, and make them want to know more.
2. Plot Twist #1—The main character is sent in a certain direction, either by accident or by another's request.
3. Development—We follow the character as he/she pursues the goal. Another character or situation is introduced to suggest a potential meeting between the two.
4. Plot Twist #2—Unexpected circumstances arise, and the main character is spun in a new direction.
5. Climax—Emotion is at its highest. The main character confronts the obstacle or antagonist designed to hinder the main character's mission.
6. Resolution—It is at this point in the story where any loose ends are tied and the character's destiny is determined.
7. Ending—The goal has been attained; the problem has been resolved; and either a conclusion has been reached or the ending is left open for the audience to decide what happens next.

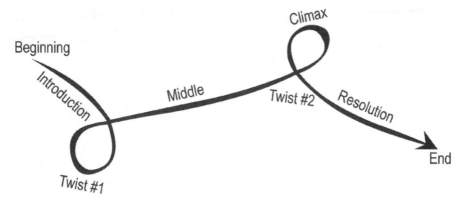

FIGURE 4-2   Diagram of a story's flow.

The following is an example of the above points applied.

The Cookie Jar

1. A young boy is sent to his room without dinner. He slowly walks upstairs, moping. Mom is angry.
2. Sitting in his room, the boy pictures the cookie jar sitting on the top shelf of the kitchen pantry. His stomach growls.
3. The boy begins to draw up plans on a big sheet of paper with designs on how to get that cookie jar without Mom knowing. He makes a list: stepladder, phone books, etc. The lights in the hallway go out. Mom's bedroom door shuts. The boy sneaks downstairs with an armful of books. He builds his stepladder and climbs aboard. Reaching out toward the jar, the books wobble, he loses his balance and falls to the floor with a loud thud, waking Mom from her slumber.
4. The lights in the upstairs hallway go on, and Mom's footsteps can be heard coming down the stairs. Quickly, the boy scurries about picking up the books, and races into the broom closet.
5. Mom enters the kitchen and suspiciously looks around. She sees nothing. She thinks perhaps the dog just knocked over the trash can again. She'll look into it in the morning. For now, she returns upstairs.
6. The boy quietly peeks out, sets down the books, and successfully reaches the cookie jar. With eyes the size of saucers, he stuffs a couple handfuls in his pajama pockets and runs upstairs to his room.

7. Beneath the covers, and flashlight in hand, the boy gobbles up his cookies while reading his comic book. Outside his room, we see a trail of cookie crumbs leading from the kitchen to the boy's room. In the final shot, we see Mom is sleeping soundly. Camera fades out.

What we have here is a rough outline listing a sequence of events using Figure 4-2 as our guide. Notice that at the very end, the audience is given a surprise, and the ending is left open for the viewer to decide what will happen next. Will the mother discover the trail of cookie crumbs and punish the boy for misbehaving? Or will the boy wake up in time to clean up the mess and escape his mother's wrath? When carefully considered, sometimes leaving an open ending can be fun for both writer and viewer.

THE SCRIPT

As the director, you control the pace at which you want the story to move and what you want the viewer to see. From the very first frame of your story, the information provided should be to illuminate and move your story forward. Once you have your characters developed and a sequence of events, it's time to fill in the details. These details can be viewed as stepping stones designed to get the audience from point 1 to point 6 in the Plot section discussed earlier.

The things you will want to think about at this stage include the following: setting, time of day, the emotional states of the characters, action, dialogue, camera movements, and transitions. In essence, you will be visualizing the film in your mind and transferring what you see onto paper. This script will then be used to make your animatic, so the more information you provide, the better.

> **TIP**
>
> To estimate the length of your film, know that one double-spaced page of type equals approximately one minute of film.

FADE IN: ————————————— Camera direction

EXT.CITY OF SUNNYDALE - NIGHT ——— Setting

A waxing blue moon overlooks the peaceful campus of Sunnydale Retirement Home.

INT. SUNNYDALE RETIREMENT HOME - DORMITORY - NIGHT

Pan across a moonlit room where several residents are asleep. Highlighted by a
small red nightlight, is a lone figure, KATHERINE GOODHUE, a.k.a. GRANNY GOODGUNS,
75, quietly loading the tubed legs of her walker with curler-shells which unbeknownst
to the audience serve as bullets to what is actually a four-barrel machine gun.

DISSOLVE TO: ————————————— Camera direction

INT.PHARMACY - NIGHT ——————— Setting   Description of scene

Matching the previous shot, DR. DOUR, 42, is also bent over quietly loading a cloth
sack with little boxes of denture adhesive. Dressed in a black lab coat, and black cap,
he is barely visible in the darkness, except for the glare of his glasses in the moonlight.
When finished, he suspiciously looks around, and tiptoes toward the exit. On his way out,
a small piece of paper falls out of his coat pocket. As he bends over to pick it up he knocks
over some bars of soap; he stops to pick them up and carefully reshelves them. Moments later,
the burglar alarm goes off.

CUT TO:

INT. SUNNYDALE RETIREMENT HOME - DORMITORY - NIGHT

Wearing camouflage flannel pajamas, Granny kisses an old family portrait on her nighstand.
Pictured are both her parents, her 6 brothers, a gray cat, and Granny when she was only
3 years old. Her father is noticeably wearing a military uniform.

                    GRANNY (sweetly) ——————— Emotional cue
                Goodnight, Mum. Goodnight Daddy.
Dialogue ———————— Goodnight Mr. Whiskers. Goodnight boys.
                Don't worry, I won't let you down.

She pulls the covers over her and retires for the night. The small red nightlight hooked
up to an outlet blinks sporadically.

CROSS DISSOLVE TO:

FIGURE 4-3   A typical page of a typed script.

Using the "Cookie Jar" plot outline as our reference, let's explore the various elements of a script.

Setting—Notice that at the very beginning of the story, the boy is sent to his room without dinner. When detailing your script, you need to decide where this scene is taking place. Are they in the living room? The backyard? In the garage? What evidence do we show to explain visually why he's being sent to his room? Is there a broken lamp on the floor? Is Mom holding his report card? Is there a dent on the car? You could even think of more fantastic ideas. What if there was a giant hole in the roof of the garage? There could be any number of reasons why his mother is upset. The more outlandish the idea, the more interesting the story.

Time of day—Sometimes the events in your outline dictate the time of day in which your story takes place. Certainly, in the Cookie Jar sample, we know it's at night because both characters are going to bed. But if your outline doesn't suggest a definite time of day, then have fun exploring the differences between the events taking place during the day versus late at night. You may be pleasantly surprised by the outcomes.

Emotional cues—As we've already established, our characters have histories and feelings that make up their personalities. The audience should be clued in to these personalities through the characters' actions and dialogue. When the boy is sent upstairs without dinner, his reaction could be anything from immediate remorse and obedience to a sudden outburst slowly waning toward acceptance. This lets us know up front if he's a respectful child or spoiled rotten.

<pre>
              DR. DOUR
       I'm sure she'll turn up.
       Can I offer you a cup of
          coffee while you wait?

              MR. LANGLEY
        Um. Are you sure this is
           the right place?

              DR. DOUR
          Cream and sugar?

Emotional cue

              MR. LANGLEY
             (suspicious)
       Actually, I think I'd better
             be going.
</pre>

FIGURE 4-4   An example of an emotional cue in a script.

Action—Spend some time observing people in real life, and you'll see that when they talk to each other, they're rarely sitting still. If in a café, you'll see someone reaching for the creamer, paying the cashier, or stirring their coffee—all in the middle of a conversation. If your character is waiting for the bus, have them tie their shoe, scratch their head, adjust the buttons on their coat, or show their eyes following a piece of trash as it blows by. Small actions like these show that the character is feeling anxious, excited, or bored. Something as simple as how a person butters her toast will show if she comes from a wealthy aristocratic background or hasn't eaten in days. In the case of our reprimanded boy, we would want to show what he is doing while sitting in his room. He could be at his desk doodling uninterestedly while his legs sway back and forth. Or he could be talking to his invisible friend. Perhaps the hole in the roof of the garage was created by this "friend" that nobody else sees but him. Again, fantasy could be at play here.

Dialogue—The most important thing to know about dialogue is to write it the way your characters would talk. Think Mark Twain versus Shakespeare. If a character is from the southern United States in the nineteenth century, their diction is completely different than someone from sixteenth-century England. Think of your character's education level and life experience as well as what part of the world they're from.

>   MONSIEUR POISSON
>   Madame. I must warn you.
>   Zee police eez not pleased.
>   Zay are steel angry about
>   last month's fiasco.
>
>
>   GRANNY
>   It's not my fault they
>   can't do their jobs.
>   They NEED me.
>
>
>
>   MONSIEUR POISSON
>   Oui, Madame. Just be careful.

FIGURE 4-5 English spoken with an over-the-top French accent.

Camera movements/angles—The camera is a powerful storytelling tool. Through a camera's movements and framing, you control the how, what, and when a viewer sees something. Here are just a few of the many camera movements that you can apply to your story.

1. Pan—Often used as an establishing shot, the camera slowly moves across the scene to create a sense of place and orient the viewer.

FIGURE 4-6   A camera pan across a village.

2. Truck in/out—When the director wants you to focus on a particular object or action, the camera will slowly push into it. This can be used to let the audience in on something that another character is not aware of. When the camera trucks out, its intention is to reveal.

FIGURE 4-7   Truck in.

3. Zoom—A sudden close-up is often used to zero in on something discovered. This quick focus creates intensity within the scene.

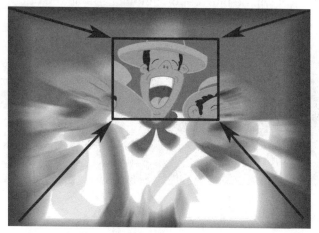

FIGURE 4-8 Zoom.

4. Dutch tilt—A slanted camera angle used to disorient the viewer and demonstrate a feeling of unease.

FIGURE 4-9 Dutch Tilt.

5. Rack focus—This technique is used when the director wants to simultaneously show you something close-up and far away within the same shot. One object will be blurred for a moment while the other is in focus.

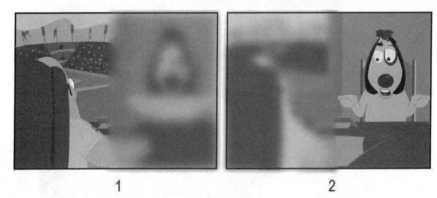

1   2

FIGURE 4-10 Rack focus.

Transitions—To go from one scene to the next, you will rely on transitions. There are many to choose from. Here are a few of the ones most commonly used.

1. Cut—The most common transition, a cut is used to show a quick passage of time. The amount of time can be short or long depending on what the next scene contains.

FIGURE 4-11 A cut from one scene to the next.

2. Dissolve—A slow transition that suggests a lengthy amount of time has passed between scenes.

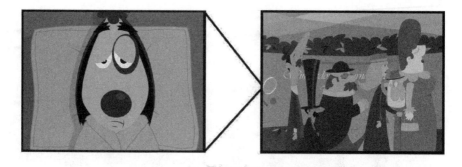

Dissolve

FIGURE 4-12   A dissolve shown in a storyboard.

3. Cross-dissolve—This transition is used artistically to match the upcoming shot with the previous shot.

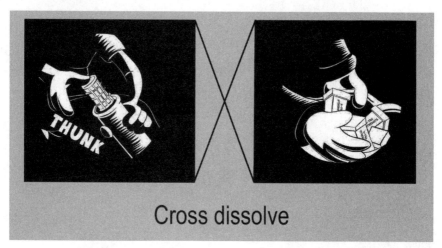

Cross dissolve

FIGURE 4-13   Indicating a cross-dissolve in a storyboard.

4. Fade in/out—To gently begin a story, you can fade into a scene from black. The transition is less jarring that way. Fading out to black and then back into the next scene can be used anywhere in the middle of a movie to show the passing of a long period of time. It is also classically used at the very end of a movie.

FIGURE 4-14   Fading to black.

SUMMARY

In this chapter, we learned how to approach an idea with an open mind and to use our imaginations to cultivate a story worth telling. We used character biographies to create the personalities of our characters and to create the worlds in which they live, and we used plot to place them in situations using storytelling devices that both capture and retain the attention of our audience. Last, we dissected a script's format and described several camera movements and techniques to use in our own projects.

EXERCISES

Exercise 4.1

Select a subject you care about, and begin brainstorming some ideas of how to communicate the message you want to come across. Expand the idea into an outline using the story arc explained in the plot section of this chapter.

Exercise 4.2

Familiarize yourself with your main characters by writing some biographies for each of them. Use these bios and the outline completed in Exercise 4.1 to move on to Exercise 4.3.

Exercise 4.3

Using your outline and biographies, type a rough draft of your script using the format demonstrated in Figure 4-2. Visualize the scenes, dialogue, actions, and camera movements in your mind and include all of the information presented in this chapter to make your story as believable and relevant to your viewer as possible.

5 Chapter IF YOU BUILD IT, THEY WILL COME

"See first that the design is wise and just: that ascertained pursue it resolutely; do not for one repulse forego the purpose that you resolved to effect."

—William Shakespeare

VISUAL DEVELOPMENT

With script in hand, we have now reached the visual development process, wherein we design our characters and backgrounds by interpreting the script visually. We accomplish this by creating concept art that will inspire the final designs of our characters and backgrounds. As mentioned briefly in Chapter 2, this is the moment where experimentation can lead to wonderful surprises. Interpreting the script literally leaves very little room for your viewer to be captivated. Your biggest challenge will be to create a visual world that complements the script in such a way that your viewer may share in the same delight watching your film as you had creating it. In other words, don't simply peer over the edge when designing at this stage; rather, take a giant leap off the edge and see what you come up with. Sometimes the more abstract or symbolic your design, the more memorable it will be. We all know what a tree looks like in reality, but your interpretation of a tree can be otherworldly. As long as the design is deliberate and consistent with the story you wish to tell, anything is possible.

FIGURE 5-1   Three interpretations of a tree.

RESEARCH

So where does one begin? Study the past. Visual storytelling has been around for thousands of years. Compare ancient Egyptian tombs and Mayan pottery to Japanese scrolls and medieval illuminated manuscripts. Every culture has its own reason for wanting to share its story. In some cases, it's to explain the journey an individual embarks on after death or to describe the typical day of its citizens. In others, it is to caution future generations about potential dangers, to pass down beliefs, or even simply to mock established order. As you study these examples, absorb as much as you can at the outset, and your voice will eventually come through. To understand how more contemporary artists have used design to share stories, visit an art museum, check out a book from your local library, or hop on the Internet and learn about the works of Vincent van Gogh, Pablo Picasso, Max Ernst, Salvador Dali, Marcel Duchamp, and Joan Miró. These artists and many others used color, texture, and design to tell their stories. The more you know about the thinking behind their work, the more you will understand their intentions. In film, you have the opportunity to use these same tools to subtly add depth to, and to define the look of, your tale.

Another artform worth researching is graphic design. This field has had a major influence on film in the past and continues to today. Some sources you may want to investigate are Chinese candy wrappers, American fruit-crate labels, Japanese toy packaging, Cuban cigar-box labels, vintage European luggage labels, pulp-fiction covers, and Mexican movie posters from the golden age of cinema. These products have all been part of their own movement in design and offer ideas on type treatment, color, and two-dimensional composition.

When you see examples that appeal to you, print them out, make copies, and paste them into a sketchbook or large art board. Arrange them by similarity of texture, color, or some other distinguishing feature. This collage of images will then become your style guide. Just as you've done with your script, add notes along the margins of your style guide to highlight how you plan to use certain elements from the collage in your film. This serves as your art direction and will facilitate the next two steps in the process.

CHARACTER DESIGN

With a full script and a character history completed, you should have a general sense of what your characters look like, and possibly sound like. This information will be indispensable as you work out the details of their costumes, interview voice actors, and plan your character's movements. But before you tackle the details, you will want to establish a certain level of consistency with your character design. Unless you have a reason to do otherwise, you want your characters to feel like they are from the same world. That's not to say that they should all look alike, but rather that they fit together nicely as a group. The key is to not get bogged down on the details, but to play with how shapes fit together. Stand your characters side by side in silhouette form, and see how they complement one another.

FIGURE 5-2   Character lineup using simple shapes.

A good starting point would be to experiment with familiar body types commonly recognized in animation, such as the barrel-chested thug with the puny head for his pea-sized brain, or the triangular-shaped hero with the tiny legs and enormous arms. There are the evil scientist with the miniature body and large egg-shaped head, the wimpy nerd with the bony arms and pencil-thin legs, and the curvy seductress with the long, flowing hair. Keep your drawings simple at this stage. Use geometric shapes for heads and bodies and lines for limbs.

FIGURE 5-3   Character lineup in silhouette form.

Once you're comfortable with their overall shapes, flesh them out a bit by drawing them as expected, and then imagine what they would look like if their personalities were actually the opposite of what we've grown accustomed to. In other words, try posing the big, hulky tough guy standing on a chair and biting his nails fearful of a tiny spider on the ground. Sometimes contradicting expectations can lead to more humorous results.

FIGURE 5-4   Character lineup with added details.

Other considerations are more stylistic. Do you prefer your characters to be angular or more curvilinear? Your line treatment could be squiggly, sketchy, or have a certain thickness. Perhaps your characters have no outline at all. The way you draw their eyes also contributes to character design consistency. Some decisions include whether to give your characters pupils or to leave just the whites of their eyes. You will want to determine what their eye shape should be (e.g., almond, circular, or oblong). Do they have eyebrows or not? Will their costumes be simplified, stylized, or heavily accessorized? Will their skin color be muted, earth-toned, or highly saturated?

FIGURE 5-5   Three varieties of character lineups.

Once you've settled on a universal appearance for your cast, you can isolate each one and work on the details based on each character's persona. A character's complexity can often be expressed by contrasting their clothes with their behavior. In the film *City Lights* starring Charlie Chaplin, the main character is a lovable tramp whose actions often contradict the stereotype one would expect of someone in his circumstance. In one scene, he stands up to a group of cruel boys who tease him to show us he has dignity. In another, while in the midst of a crisis (he has a sword stuck in his pants), he instantly pauses to honor the national anthem to show us he is respectful. Walking past a store window, he stops to admire a work of art to show that he appreciates the finer things in life. Regardless of the trouble he finds himself in, his vest is always buttoned, showing us that he is proud. We also learn that, ironically, he does not like the taste of liquor, thus shattering any preconceived notions we might have about him. And yet, we are always reminded that he is a tramp, because his clothes do not fit right, his pants have holes in them, and his shoes are too big. Because that all humans have contradictions, we can very easily identify with him. If your characters can achieve the same level of empathy, you've taken a huge step toward luring your viewer into your world.

BACKGROUND DESIGN

A background says a lot about the characters that inhabit it. The background stories you assembled earlier contain clues about each character's environment. As you read through these biographies, ask yourself what types of things each character would value. People tend to surround themselves with things that bring them comfort. Many people even collect objects with which they can relate. Your characters are no different. If you approach backgrounds as characters, they, too, can come alive and help tell your story by establishing a mood with color and providing information through strategically placed details. Imagine for a moment a disheveled man, alone in a musty apartment, lit only by a single bulb and a thin ray of moonlight sneaking in through the blinds of his living room window. At this point, we really don't know much about him because we have no point of reference. Hang a portrait on the wall of him as a young, successful Hollywood actor, and the audience will begin to put the puzzle pieces together. How he went from one point in his life to another is a question that will be answered as your story unfolds, either confirming or astonishing your audience. Either way, watching your film just went from being a passive activity to an interactive one. What better way to hold someone's interest?

FIGURE 5-6   Establish your setting with mood and details.

It's possible that the background could even tell a story within the main story. Often, this is illustrated in children's books with details carefully placed throughout the scene. Children will reread books countless times because they discover something new each time. Your film could have that same element of discovery through the use of symbolism and motif.

Visual metaphors, also known as symbols or motifs, are elements contained within your setting to enhance the story by subtle means. Suppose the story deals with the issue of miscommunication, and your protagonist tries desperately to connect with another character in the story with little success. Some symbolic imagery you could include in your background might be bridges in the distance, a small spider spinning its web in the corner of a room, a billboard for a cell-phone company on a passing bus, or a baby crying for its milk next door. Each one of these details can be used to subconsciously reinforce the main character's attempt to reach out and connect with the other.

The nice thing about having your characters and plot already established is that your story will naturally lend itself to certain locations. As a result, additional details like those mentioned above will logically fall into place. Compare a fairy tale set in a rain forest to one situated in a busy metropolis, and you can see how each environment will dictate its own opportunities for allegory.

Rainforest	City	Symbolic Possibilities
Tree canopies	Skyscrapers	Grandeur
River	Water fountain	Life
Tree trunks	Brick buildings	Stability
Dirt path	Concrete walkways	Journey
Leaves blowing	Crowded subway	Activity
Flowers	Children	Hope
Bones	Trash	Consumption
Monkeys	Cars	Noise
Fire ants	Alleyways	Danger

FIGURE 5-7 Every location offers ingredients for symbolism.

Of course, thinking of creative ways to support your story does not have to be limited to visuals. The baby crying next door, for instance, uses sound.

We will cover the topic of sound in more detail later in the book, but in the meantime take note that sound can include anything from background music to environmental sounds like thunder, wind, or city traffic. How scary would most horror movies be without music to build up the intensity or a blast of thunder at just the right moment?

Use Reference

The nice thing about being a filmmaker in this day and age is that if you're not sure what a Mediterranean hydrofoil looks like, you can instantly find one on the Internet and redraw it in the style of your animated film. Sure, it would be nice to take a trip down to Greece and ride one yourself, but hey, we've got a film to make here. On the other hand, if what you're looking for is within reach, then a better option would be to go see it for yourself and take a few minutes to copy it in a sketchbook. If that's not an option, snap a picture.

FIGURE 5-8   Photographic reference.

When copying photographs, the trick is not to literally copy what you see, but rather to boil the object down to its essence and interpret that into a design that suits your needs. A camera captures everything within its frame, including things that may have nothing to do with the feeling of your film. Notice that I use the term "feeling" when referring to your film. That's because your goal is to extract an emotion from your audience. If the scene is warm and inviting, then it might call for a close-up shot of an intimate setting with lots of wood, warm colors, and delicate patterns. On the other hand, if a particular scene is intended to make your character feel insignificant, then his/her surroundings should emphasize that point using a long shot of cold, bare, concrete walls, sharp angles, steep curves, dark colors, bold patterns, and the use of scale and composition. Your character isn't the only one who should feel insignificant in the film. Your audience should too. Make them participants, not just casual observers. As the designer, you have the responsibility to set the tone for your film, so it's to your advantage to exaggerate your motifs as much as possible to ensure that the emotion comes across clearly.

FIGURE 5-9 Sketching on location.

TWO-DIMENSIONAL COMPOSITION AND DESIGN

You should approach your background settings just as you did when initially designing your characters—by defining their overall shapes. In the case of your backgrounds, your aim is twofold: to strike a visual balance between the objects in your scene and to create a focal point as a way of directing the viewer's eye. Fortunately, most of the hard work has already been done for you because many of the world's master painters have already established several successful compositions through centuries of experimentation and study. Let's look at a few of these compositions in thumbnail form and examine how they work.

Your stage in Adobe® Flash® can be divided into nine equal parts. The points at which these lines intersect are considered to be pleasing to the eye, thus they are prime locations for your focal points.

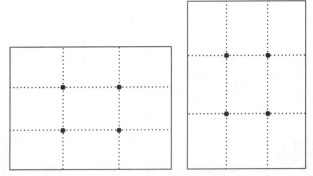

FIGURE 5-10   A horizontal and vertical canvas, each with four focal points from which to choose.

This first example leads the viewer's eye along a curvilinear path that can either be directly drawn or implied through the placement of other objects in the scene. The focus can be anywhere near or on the path.

FIGURE 5-11   Leading the eye with a dominant "S" curve.

The silhouette acts like a picture frame, enclosing your subject. Examples of commonly used frames include tunnels, archways, stairwells, trees, windows, etc.

FIGURE 5-12   Using silhouette to frame your focal point.

As we've already learned, one-point perspective relies heavily on parallel lines going away from you and meeting at one point. This next example works similarly to direct the eye toward your subject.

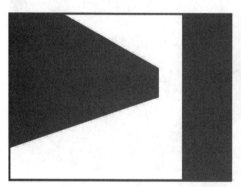 

FIGURE 5-13   Providing direction with a strong diagonal.

By abutting dark colors against light colors, you can use contrasting values to lead the eye through your scene toward your intended target.

FIGURE 5-14   Applying tonal contrast (lights against darks) to create depth.

Clustering elements in your scene is more appealing and less mechanical than spacing objects evenly throughout. Look to nature for examples of interesting clusters: leaves on a tree, schools of fish, stars in the sky, plants in the ocean, even people at a party.

FIGURE 5-15   Clusters used to direct the eye and create balance on a page.

When discussing balance, we don't literally mean two objects of the same size placed side by side. This would cause your composition to flatten out, giving the opposite of the effect we are trying to achieve. Rather, you are looking to create a balance between positive and negative space, so the human eye can register what to look at first, second, and third. This is called the principle of threes.

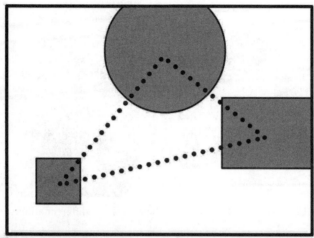

FIGURE 5-16 Using the principle of threes to create a balance.

A simple but powerful method to grab someone's attention is to make your subject different from its surroundings. For example, picture a pink flamingo in a colony of penguins.

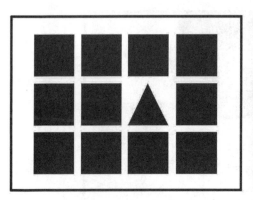 

FIGURE 5-17   Calling attention through shape differentiation.

As you study the examples shown above, imagine specific scenes in your own script, and quickly sketch out some possibilities. Remember to keep your sketches small so you're not distracted by unnecessary details this early in the design process.

Background Layout

As you continue to experiment with various compositions for your film, some things to think about include the number of backgrounds needed, the staging of your characters within the scene, the most effective camera angle for telling the story, continuity of cuts from scene to scene, and how camera movement affects the mood of the scene.

Reusing Backgrounds

Review your script once again, and note any sequences that take place in the same location—you may be able to draw one large layout and use different portions throughout the film. A shift in camera position may be all you need to add variety, thus sparing you from having to draw individual backgrounds for every single scene in your film.

FIGURE 5-18 A sample layout indicating how the camera will move as it follows the character. This one layout contains enough information to be used repeatedly using a mixture of far
shots and close-ups.

STAGING

Once you've decided on an overall composition, it's time to place the additional
elements within the scene that are going to reinforce your message. If the scene
is an abandoned warehouse that has been neglected for quite some time, draw
some cobwebs, broken pipes, random puddles of water, roof shingles on the
floor, stacks of boxes, rusty railings, broken staircases, and cracked windows.
Be sure to draw each object in its entirety, even if a portion of the object is
obscured in the final layout. By drawing the object, or asset, completely, you
have the freedom to move it around the scene with ease and scale it up or down
as needed without fear of exposing a missing piece.

FIGURE 5-19   Assets not drawn in their entirety are susceptible to revealing mistakes if relocated.

Let's break down what a layout looks like in different stages.

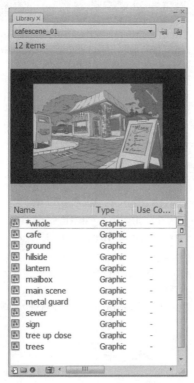

FIGURE 5-20   All items drawn are stored in your **Library** once they have been converted to symbols. Simply select each item, and drag it onto your stage.

FIGURE 5-21   Assets randomly placed on the stage, ready for distribution and compositing.

FIGURE 5-22   All assets have been distributed to layers and put into place.

As an exercise let's create a few assets, convert them to symbols, and distribute them to layers.

1. Open a new file with the following settings: 720 × 540, 30 fps.

2. Draw some assets (three will suffice) in their entirety, using any of the techniques described in Chapter 3. See an example in Figure 5-23 below.

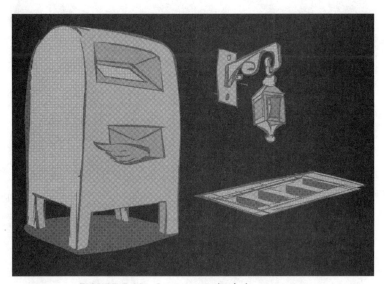

FIGURE 5-23   Some assets in their raw states.

3. Use either the **Selection** tool or the **Lasso** tool to select one of the assets. With the asset selected, press **F8** on your keyboard, or go to **Modify/ Convert to Symbol**. Name the symbol something recognizable. Select **Graphic**, leave the registration point in the center, and click **OK**.

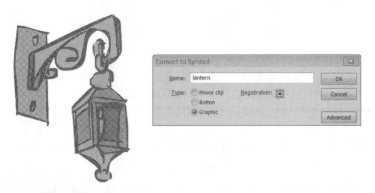

FIGURE 5-24   The **Convert to Symbol** pop-up panel.

4. Repeat steps 1–3 for all of the remaining assets.

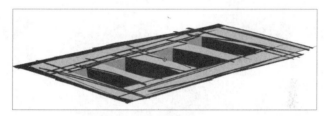

FIGURE 5-25   Your new symbol as it appears on Scene 1.

When selecting your new symbols, you will see that they are now contained within a blue box and can easily be moved around the stage. Notice, however, that they are all on the same layer. This would be a problem should you decide to animate some of them (to simulate a camera pan, for instance). For this reason, we must distribute each symbol to its own layer. Let's do so now.

1. Use the **Selection** tool to drag across the stage, and select all of the symbols.
2. Hover over one of the selected symbols and right-click. Scroll down to **Distribute to Layers**.

FIGURE 5-26 The **Distribute to Layers** command.

Your symbols are now in their proper layers and are named accordingly.

What if you accidentally delete a symbol from your stage? Can you get it back? The answer is, "Absolutely." Let's try it.

3. Select all of the symbols on your stage either by dragging across the stage or dragging down the keyframes in your timeline. Tap **Delete** on your keyboard. Your stage and all of the keyframes should be empty. To retrieve the assets, open your **Library (Ctrl+L)** or **Window ▶ Library**. You should see all of your symbols neatly arranged, just as you named them.

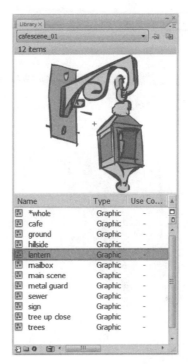

FIGURE 5-27   Your **Library**'s assets.

4. Drag several copies of different symbols onto your stage so that you have multiple "instances" as shown below.

FIGURE 5-28   Multiple instances of different symbols on the stage.

5. Double-click on one of the symbols to go inside the symbol, and make a drastic change to the drawing.

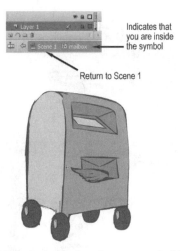

Indicates that you are inside the symbol

Return to Scene 1

FIGURE 5-29   An indication that you are inside a symbol.

6. When you're through, return to Scene 1 by clicking on **Scene 1** just below the tiny trash-can icon.

FIGURE 5-30   Returning to the main scene.

You are once again outside of the symbol. Notice that all of the instances have been affected, including the one inside your library. That's because they all share the same name.

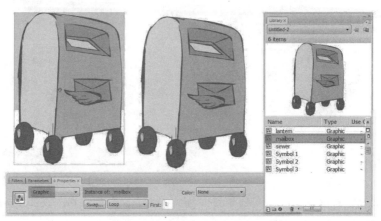

FIGURE 5-31 All affected instances, the **Properties** panel, and the original symbol in the library.

7. Select one of the affected symbols on your stage and right-click. Scroll down to **Duplicate Symbol**. Give this symbol a different name, and click **OK**.

FIGURE 5-32 The **Duplicate Symbol** pop-up panel.

8. Double-click on the symbol to go inside and make another drastic change. When complete, return to the main scene (Scene 1). Since this symbol has a different instance name, none of the other symbols were affected by this change.

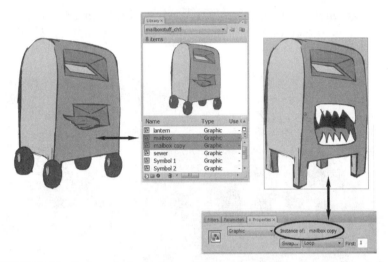

FIGURE 5-33 Each symbol with its own instance name in the **Properties** panel.

9. Look at your **Library** again. You should see your newest symbol along with the others.

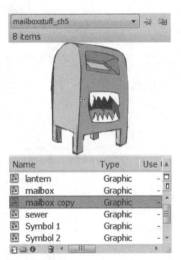

FIGURE 5-34 The newly added symbol in the **Library**.

You can now confidently begin laying out your backgrounds, building assets, and placing them in your scene. As you do so, remember to leave enough room within the composition for your characters to interact without being obstructed from view. Your character's gestures should read clearly.

Camera

The best camera angle is the one that reinforces the action taking place at that moment. If your goal is to accentuate isolation, try placing the camera above and away looking down at the character. If you want to show a character's authority, place the camera low so that the audience is looking up at him.

Camera 1   Camera 2   Camera 3

FIGURE 5-35   How do you show a character trying to grasp something just out of reach? Here are three possibilities. Can you think of others?

See Figure 5-36 for some common camera views and their related uses.

Full Shot - Establishes character within the scene. The audience is an observer.

Medium Shot - Allows the audience to read the character's body gestures while listening to their dialogue.

Close up - Very personal. Creates a direct connection with the viewer.

Extreme Close up - Creates intensity and unease.

FIGURE 5-36   Straight-on shots and what they mean.

Continuity

Lack of continuity from one scene to the next can be disorienting to the viewer. Make sure that if a character exits screen right in one scene, you show them entering from the left in the following scene. Otherwise, it will be unclear where he/she came from. It's just as important to know where your characters are when cutting back and forth from one to another. See Figure 5-37 below for a means to ensure that your characters are always on the correct side of the screen.

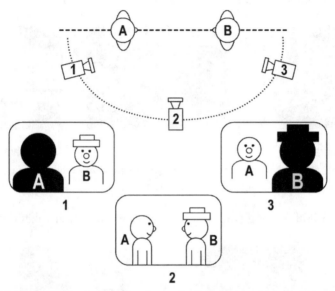

FIGURE 5-37 Continuity requires keeping each character on the same side of the screen.

In the diagram above, you can see that each character will remain on the same side of the screen no matter where you place the camera, as long as it is only allowed to rotate on a 180° curve. The moment the camera crosses the line over to the other side, continuity will be lost.

Pacing

The movement of your camera can also be used to set a mood within the picture. A slow pan, for example, eases the viewer into a scene peacefully, whereas a zip (faster) pan is more unsettling. Trucking in toward your character's face may suggest a somber mood, but a zoom into someone's eyes creates tension. Be deliberate about your camera's position and about how it moves around the scene. This will strengthen your story.

COLOR THEORY

Another storytelling device is color. Like symbols, color can be used to give underlying meaning to your film. The key is to use restraint. Rather than apply every color in the rainbow, you want to limit your palette to three or four colors, maximum. This will permit you to keep a unified appearance. But even then, determining which colors to use can be a daunting task. A simple approach is to pick two colors similar in nature and one color completely different from the others. This ensures that you have a dominant color scheme in your composition, with the accent color serving as your focal point. One way to think about it is in how people dress: A man might be wearing a dark suit jacket and dark slacks, but highlight it with a vibrantly colored tie; a woman may wear a subdued dress with matching shoes, and accentuate it with a brightly colored scarf. The main outfit is the dominant color with the accents acting as focal points.

To help you make your choices, it's important to know how the eye sees color. As a general rule, warm colors advance in a picture, while cool colors recede into the distant void. Examples of warm colors are yellow, yellow-orange, orange, orange-red, red, and red-violet. Cool colors include yellow-green, green, green-blue, blue, blue-violet, and violet. Of course, a slight shift in each hue can cause a color to go from warm to cool, or vice versa, but this is a good place to start. Examples in the real world exist everywhere you go. To grab your attention, stop signs are red, road signs are yellow, street cones are orange. Serving as backdrops are green hills, yellow-green grass, and blue sky. Look out your window on a cloudy, rainy day, and you'll notice some other truths about color. Sidewalks, streets, and parking lots get darker and blend into one another. White cars, white buses, and bright yellow taxicabs will pop forward. A two-dimensional composition works the same way. On a neutral background, the dark objects will move back and the lighter colors will come forward. You will also notice that the closer an object is to you, the richer its color, and the more crisp its lines and details appear. Look at buildings far off into the distance, and you'll see that atmosphere begins to soften their edges and dull their color. The contrast between those buildings and their background is significantly less.

Color Meanings

Colors mean different things to different people, and the differences can be significant between cultures, but there are some meanings that most people can agree on with regard to color. Here are a few common colors with their respective associations.

Yellow	Energy, vitality, sunshine, youth, lemon, tart, dry.
Purple	Royalty, stability, elegance, intelligent, flamboyant.
Blue	Sorrow, tranquil, vacation, cold, freedom.
Orange	Warm, friendly, cheerful, alarm, drab.
Green	Sickly, fresh, envy, nature, calm.
Red	Danger, heat, loud, bold, passion, excitement.
White	Pure, sporty, delicate, fluffy, plain.
Black	Elegance, death, fear, mystery.

FIGURE 5-38   Colors and their meanings.

Looking at Figure 5-38 above, you can see that one color can have a multitude of meanings, and some may even contradict others. That's because for the most part, the meaning one gives to a color is subjective, and with millions of colors to pick from, it's impossible to find one color that means the same thing to all people. Take the color blue for example. A light baby blue leaves a very different impression than a deep, dark blue. Add to that the fact that a color's meaning can be altered when combined with another color, and you'll discover that the best solution is to opt for hues that have meaning to you. So, experiment freely with different color combinations until you find the ones that speak clearly. Your audience will be more likely to connect with you when those choices have been made consciously. For inspiration, look at magazines on fashion and interior design. Rent movies that have won awards for their art direction and study their lighting by pausing on individual frames. Spend an afternoon at an art museum, and note how focal points were created through clever use of color. Color is everywhere.

Color Palette and Mood

Now that we know a little about the psychology of colors, we can use that to determine our palette. If you think of color in Adobe Flash as lighting in a live-action film, then you open yourself up to "light" your scenes according to the mood you wish to set for any particular sequence. If the scene is dark and morose, then you would choose a palette to reflect that. If a later sequence is humorous and uplifting, you can then switch to another palette. As with your character and background designs, consistency is what will hold your film together, thus freeing you up to approach color as another tool to help tell your story.

FIGURE 5-39   Mood and temperature compared.

To quickly establish a mood for your scenes, it's best to translate your existing background layouts into small thumbnail sketches and "block" in broad strokes of color. The reason for making these sketches small is to avoid being distracted by details. These thumbnails serve a second purpose: to help direct the attention of the viewer to a specific area within the composition. For example, the overall color scheme of the room could be cool blue and green colors. The area you want people to concentrate on could then be a bright, warm color. Try this using the large paintbrush and set the stage to a size no larger than an index card.

FIGURE 5-40   A quick color study in thumbnail form to highlight point of interest.

ASSEMBLING A LIBRARY

As you have already seen, the Adobe® Flash® library is a great tool for reusing symbols, making adjustments to several symbols simultaneously, and duplicating symbols for minor adjustments. This is a great time-saver as long as you can find the assets you're looking for. Over time, however, your library will grow, and it can potentially store hundreds of symbols. Without some organization along the way, locating an asset is like finding the proverbial needle in the haystack. Luckily, there are two things you can do to keep a tidy library: (1) set up a naming convention for your symbols, and (2) categorize assets in specific folders.

One good approach to naming your assets is to include the date in which you created it. This way, if you have more than one car in your film, their difference will be noted by the date. Another element to include in the name would be the sequence in which that asset is used. So if you have a car in the city and another in the country, their names will indicate that. Finally, you can add a specific attribute to differentiate one symbol from another. So a red car in the city made on October 17, 2009, could be named 101709_city_car_red, and a blue car in the country made on June 8, 2010, could be named 060810_country_car_blue.

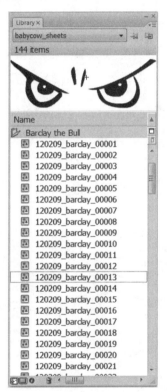

FIGURE 5-41   A naming convention applied to several symbols in a library.

The reason for this naming convention is twofold. First of all, Adobe Flash organizes your assets alphabetically, so if you have a general idea of when you created an asset, the date will assist you in locating it. Secondly, by including the sequence in the name, you can arrange your folders by sequence, thus matching the labels in your storyboards and making it even easier to find the asset you are looking for. More information on storyboards is provided in Chapter 6.

New Symbol

New Folder

FIGURE 5-42 Folders in the library categorized by locations and characters.

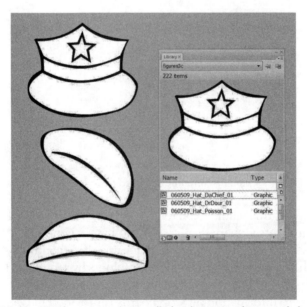

FIGURE 5-43 Naming convention applied to hats worn by several characters.

CHARACTER RIGGING VIA SYMBOLS

As you build your characters, imagine them in motion. Even something as simple as a dog running can have several parts in motion concurrently. Ears will flop up and down, the tail will wag, the tongue can sway, all while all four legs are moving about. With this in mind, you will want to convert each movable part into its own symbol, and eventually give it its own layer. See the enclosed Adobe Flash file named **tennisball.fla** for a sample animation containing several assets in motion simultaneously.

FIGURE 5-44   Body parts separated and united.

It's good practice to always draw your characters, props, and other assets at the size they are intended to be used in the Adobe Flash file. Otherwise, you may encounter problems with scaling as you begin to nest your symbols later in the animation process. Nesting symbols will be covered in Chapter 7.

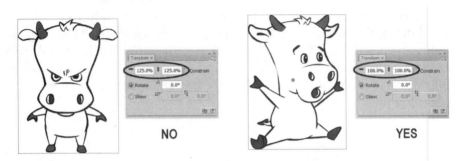

FIGURE 5-45 Ensure that all assets are at 100% their size before converting to symbols.

Layering Body Parts

Rigging your characters for animation is an exciting process because you are beginning to see them come to life. Eventually, you will become so proficient that certain tasks in the building process will become routine. Unfortunately, this can sometimes lead to a temporary lack of concentration, and there may be times when you forget to delete things you don't need. To be sure that there are no stragglers on the stage, temporarily convert all of your layers into outlines to see if there are any symbols hiding underneath other symbols. Delete or move them as necessary.

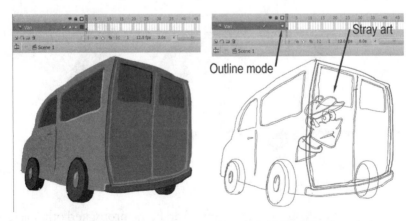

FIGURE 5-46 Outlining layers reveal symbols hiding behind symbols.

Once all of the body parts have been drawn and converted to symbols, you can use the same technique described in Figure 5-26 to distribute them to their own layers.

FIGURE 5-47   Body parts distributed to layers.

The Eight-Point Turnaround

Knowing how your characters look from several angles and in different poses will not only provide you with a visual portrayal of your characters' personalities, but you will also save time in the long run, because every drawing you make becomes an additional asset stored in your library for later use. Let's begin with an eight-point turnaround.

Assuming that the lineup you created earlier in this chapter uses the front view, you already have one of the eight views needed to complete the turnaround. The others are the left- and right-side views, two three-quarter front views, two three-quarter rear views, and a rear view. The nice thing about working digitally is that once you have created one side view, to make the other side view you simply select the character using the **Selection** tool, press **Ctrl+d** on your keyboard to duplicate it, and go to **Modify ▶Transform ▶Flip Horizontal**, or more simply, use the shortcut key we set up earlier in the book and tap **/** (forward slash key) on your keyboard. Voila! You now have both side views complete. The same can be done for both three-quarter views.

As you draw the additional views, you should set up some horizontal guidelines to ensure that the character's body parts line up properly as the character turns. See Figure 5-48 for their proper placement.

FIGURE 5-48   Using guidelines for proper alignment.

To access the guidelines in Adobe Flash, you must first make the rulers visible by going to **View ▶Rulers**.

FIGURE 5-49   Rulers accessible via the **View** drop-down menu.

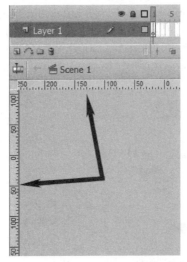

FIGURE 5-50   Your horizontal and vertical rulers.

Once they become visible, click anywhere on the ruler and drag down to create a guideline. Repeat as needed, and move them into place anywhere on the stage.

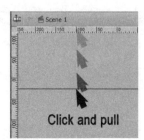

FIGURE 5-51   Dragging a guideline down from the ruler.

The Model Sheet

The purpose of the model sheet is to show how the character acts and reacts in various circumstances through body gesture and pose. Often, animation is more effective at expressing a character's emotions when poses and gestures are exaggerated through a line of action. Compare the poses in Figure 5-52 to see how exaggeration can really help sell an emotion. Be sure to refer back to your eight-point turnaround for the correct proportions. "Staying on model" is important for consistency. Otherwise, your character will slowly morph into a completely different character over time.

FIGURE 5-52   Use a line of action and sculpt your pose around it to give your character more personality.

FIGURE 5-53 A typical model sheet.

Expression Sheets

Facial expressions are another way to gauge how your character is feeling. Choose from any number of emotions like joy, disgust, fear, shock, envy, disappointment, sorrow, confusion, mischief, anger, and any others you can think of. Remember to exaggerate.

Expressions Sheet
Date: _____

FIGURE 5-54   A typical expression sheet.

TEXTURES

So far, our focus has been on creating and preparing two-dimensional vector art for animation. Those of you who know how to paint in Adobe® Photoshop® and are familiar with its layers, however, have the option of creating textured raster art and importing that into Adobe Flash as well. If you have a layered Adobe Photoshop file handy, this is how you would bring it into Adobe Flash.

1. First open a new document set at 720 × 540 pixels, and 30 fps.
2. From the top menu bar, choose **File ▶Import ▶Import to Stage** and locate your layered .PSD file. Click **Open**.
3. A pop-up window will appear, offering you the option to choose which layers you wish to import. Check the ones that apply. Click **OK**.

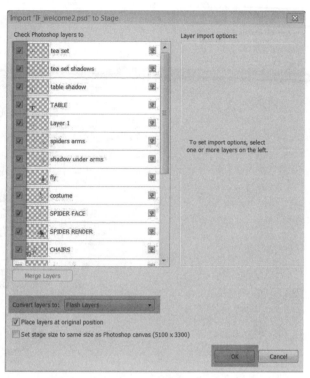

FIGURE 5-55   Importing a layered .PSD file.

4. That's all there is to it. Your painting will be imported just as it appeared in the original Adobe Photoshop file. The separate layers allow you to animate characters and objects freely within the scene, moving behind and in front of the imported assets. This is a great way to combine vector and raster.

FIGURE 5-56   The imported Adobe® Photoshop® file.

If you're not familiar with Adobe Photoshop, but would still like to incorporate some texture in your projects, you're in luck. Let's apply a blur and texture to some movie clips to create smoke rising from a brick-textured chimney. Remember to always save (**Ctrl+S**) your documents frequently as you work on them, just in case your computer crashes or the program freezes. For this exercise, simply save it to your desktop.

1. First open a new document in Adobe Flash set at 720 × 540 pixels, and 30 fps.
2. Draw a simple chimney and convert the pieces into symbols. When converting to symbols (**F8**), name each piece and choose **Movie Clip** as the type.

FIGURE 5-57   Vector drawing waiting for texture to be applied.

3. Locate a texture you like (many sites online offer free textures for download).
4. Import the texture into Adobe Flash by going to **File ▶Import ▶Import to Library**.

FIGURE 5-58   Import drop-down menu.

5. The texture is now located in two places: your **Library**, and the **Color** panel.

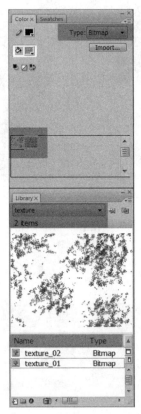

FIGURE 5-59   Locations of imported textures.

6. Double-click inside the symbol you wish to texture, and open the **Color** panel. From the **Color** panel, choose **Bitmap** from the **Type** drop-down menu. The new texture will replace the original color. To give this texture a background color, create a second layer below the original layer, and fill it with a color.

FIGURE 5-60   Choose **Bitmap** from the **Type** drop-down menu.

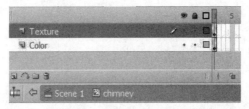

FIGURE 5-61   **Texture** and **Color** layers inside the main symbol.

7. You can play with various color effects by selecting the symbol, clicking on the **Color** menu in the **Properties** panel and choosing **Advanced ▶Settings**.

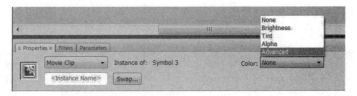

FIGURE 5-62   The **Properties** panel **Advanced** tab.

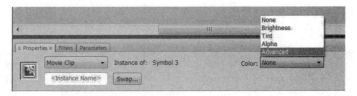

FIGURE 5-63   The **Advanced Effect** pop-up panel.

8. Customize to your heart's desire.

FIGURE 5-64 The textured house completed.

9. Now let's set up a movie clip containing a simple animation of smoke rising from the chimney. With a white-filled paint brush, draw a squiggle. Convert that to a symbol, and choose **Movie Clip** for the type. Name it **Animated Smoke**.

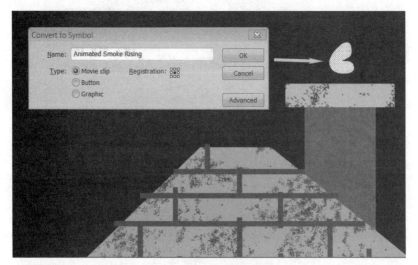

FIGURE 5-65 Squiggle converted to a **Movie Clip** for animation purposes.

10. Double-click on the symbol to go inside the **Animated Smoke** symbol. Notice that on the timeline it is occupying one keyframe. Let's make a few more. Every three frames, press **F6** on your keyboard, or go to **Insert ▶Timeline ▶Keyframe**. Repeat this step six times. (See the file named **texture.fla** in the enclosed DVD for reference.)

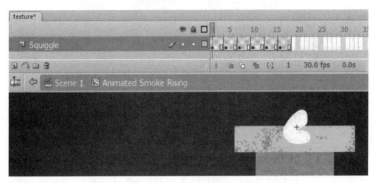

FIGURE 5-66   Six keyframes added to the timeline ready to be animated.

11. Select each keyframe (black dot) from the timeline and use the **Selection** tool to move the squiggle up a few pixels on the stage. Repeat this action for the rest of the keyframes.
12. After adjusting each keyframe, pull the red scrubber bar along the timeline to see the animation.

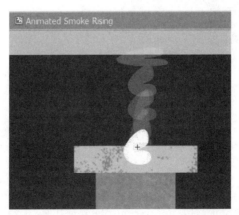

FIGURE 5-67   The different stages of the smoke rising.

13. To complete the effect, we will add a blur to the movie clip. Click on **Scene 1** to return to the main timeline. Select the animated movie clip, and open the **Properties** panel. Click on the **Filters** tab.

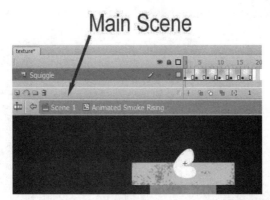

FIGURE 5-68 Returning to the main timeline.

14. Press and hold the **+** (plus) symbol and choose **Blur** to add the filter. Adjust the sliders as needed. You can see that I chose **40** with the **Quality** set to **Medium**.

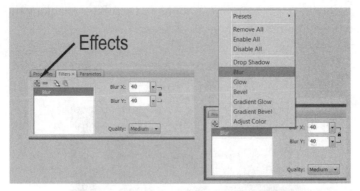

FIGURE 5-69 Adding special effects from the **Filters** tab.

15. Deselect the symbol by clicking anywhere on the stage. From the top menu bar, choose **Control ▶ Test Movie**. A new window will pop up on your screen with the animation playing. This window is called a **.swf** (pronounced "swiff"), and will place a .swf file on your desktop next to the original .fla file. Each time you test your movie, the .swf will be updated,

FIGURE 5-39   Mood and temperature compared.

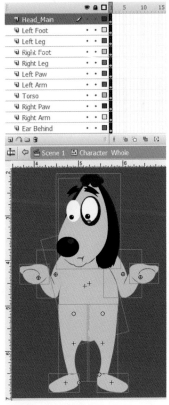

FIGURE 5-47   Body parts distributed to layers.

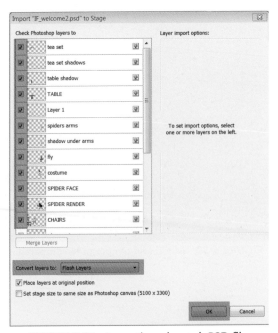

FIGURE 5-55   Importing a layered .PSD file.

FIGURE 5-56 The imported Adobe® Photoshop® file.

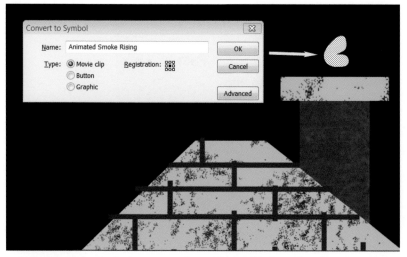

FIGURE 5-65 Squiggle converted to a **Movie Clip** for animation purposes.

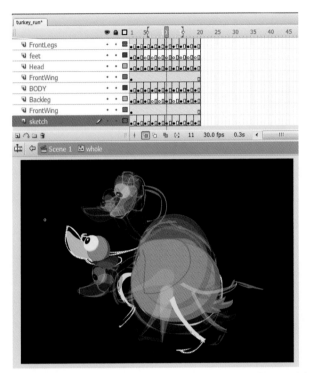

FIGURE 7-11 Use the **Onion Skin Tool** to preview drawings preceding and following your current frame.

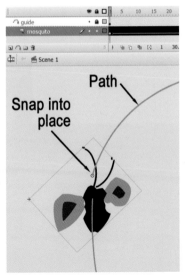

FIGURE 7-14 Snap each symbol to the two endpoints of the loop.

FIGURE 7-23 The outline and fill separated into two layers.

FIGURE 7-24 Creating the mask for the gears.

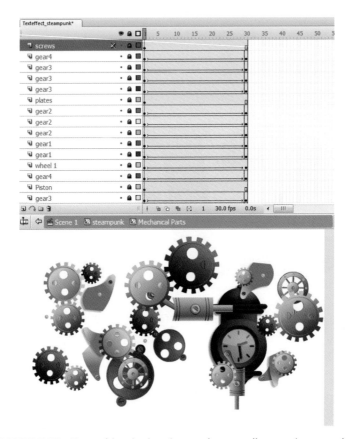

FIGURE 7-27 Every object is given its own layer to allow motion tweening.

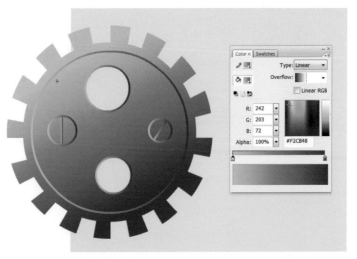

FIGURE 7-29 The gradient settings used to create a gold metallic effect.

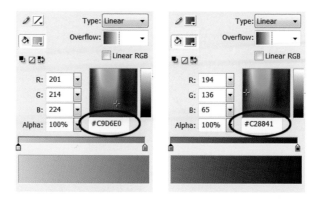

Silver   Copper

FIGURE 7-30   Gradient settings for silver and copper.

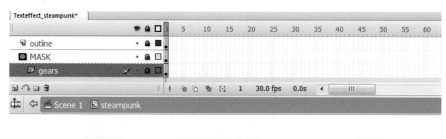

FIGURE 7-31   Checking the arrangement of the gears within the letters.

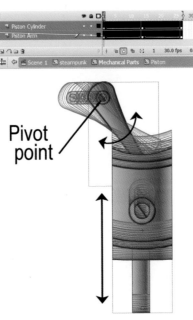

FIGURE 7-33 Rotating the piston's parts on individual layers. Movement shown via Onion Skin Outlines.

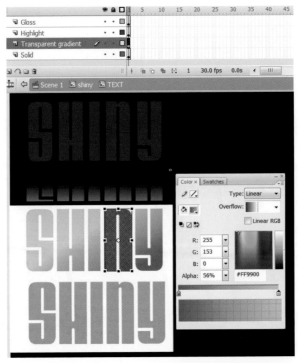

FIGURE 7-42 Layers named and a breakdown of how each layer has been affected.

allowing you to play it from your desktop by double-clicking it with your mouse. Close the window, and pat yourself on the back for completing your first animation.

SUMMARY

At the heart of this chapter lie the lessons needed to translate words into pictures. By taking our script's cues, we were able to build our worlds and the characters that inhabit them. We learned that clear communication begins with a strong two-dimensional composition, is reinforced with proper use of color and camera selection, and is solidified with purposeful character design and dynamic posing and gesture. We discovered the importance of maintaining an organized file, and we prepped a character for animation by converting assets to symbols and distributing them to layers. Finally, we expanded our artistic options by including textured assets from outside sources.

EXERCISES

Exercise 5.1

FIGURE 5-70   Clothes say a lot about a person.

Mix and match the descriptions listed below with an animal and draw what that character would look like. Give them costumes to reflect their personalities.

Descriptions

1. A messy, eccentric with a friendly disposition
2. A free spirit with a sordid past
3. A handsome but arrogant narcissist
4. A wise but stingy penny-pincher

Animals

1. A fox
2. An otter
3. A rat
4. A squirrel

Exercise 5.2

Take photographs of some neighborhood landmarks in the early morning, afternoon, evening, and night. These landmarks can be anything from a statue in the park to a bus stop. The important thing is to take the pictures from the same angle for each time of day. Upload the photos to a new document in Adobe Flash, place them side by side on the stage, and soak up the colors for each picture, saving each set as its own color palette. Compare the differences from each palette by drawing a thumbnail sketch of a simple scene and coloring it with each set.

Exercise 5.3

Pick a scene from your script, and find an existing painting that reflects a similar mood. A good starting point for reference might be to delve into the works of Henri Matisse, Jean-Michel Basquiat, Joan Miró, Claude Monet, and Wassily Kandinsky. Scan a picture of this painting and import the scan into Adobe Flash. Soak up the colors from the painting using the **Eyedropper** tool and save these colors as a new color palette. Design a background for one of your scenes using these colors.

Chapter 6
WHAT YOU SEE IS WHAT YOU GET

"A film is never really good unless the camera is an eye in the head of a poet."

—Orson Welles

THE STORYBOARD

As mentioned in Chapter 2, a storyboard helps determine the staging of your characters and props, the posing of your characters, camera movements, and scene transitions, and the overall timing with the use of dialogue and/or music. That's a big task, but in the end you will have the closest incarnation of your film to date. Putting together a detailed storyboard is a full-time job that larger production companies can afford to staff. Typically, the storyboard artist will show how the characters act within each scene by indicating every gesture moment by moment. Since we intend to do the work ourselves, it's more efficient for us to make a storyboard that highlights key moments in each scene, with one main gesture to convey the overall mood of that scene. This will give us the freedom to "act out" the gestures during the rough animation process.

Let's break down everything that goes into a typical storyboard. Referring to Figure 6-1, you can see that a storyboard is made up of a series of boxes and lines with room to fill in the blanks. Each section indicates where you are in the film, what is happening, what you're listening to, and what will happen next.

DATE: __/__/____   PRODUCTION: _____   CREATED BY: _____   PAGE #:_____

| SEQ. | SCENE | PANEL | BG | | SEQ. | SCENE | PANEL | BG | | SEQ. | SCENE | PANEL | BG |

ACTION

DIALOGUE

TRANSITION

NOTES

FIGURE 6-1   A blank storyboard.

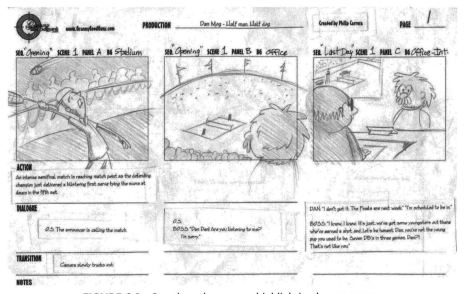

FIGURE 6-2   Storyboard sequence highlighting key moments.

At the very top of the page, you will write the date you worked on that page, the name of your film, show or presentation, your name, and the page number. Above each rectangle, you will indicate the name of each sequence, the number of the scene and panel, and the background you'll be using (this was determined during the layout stage covered in Chapter 5). Below are brief descriptions of how each element works.

Sequence—The title of each sequence can be derived from the script. If your film begins with a man and a woman arguing while seated at a café, the sequence can be called "The Argument" and will remain so until the audience is transported elsewhere.

Scene—Every time you cut from one scene to another, you must indicate this with a new drawing. Using the couple in the café as our example, if scene 1 shows a medium shot of the man gesturing wildly and the camera cuts to a close-up of the woman rolling her eyes, this next shot is scene 2. If we cut back to the man knocking over his coffee cup, this is scene 3. Cut to an extreme close-up of the espresso machine steaming milk, and you are at scene 4.

Panel—Panels show the continuation of action within a scene. Pulling the camera slightly back from the steaming espresso machine, imagine a shot of the barista's hands removing the pitcher, cleaning the nozzle, and adding a dollop of foam to the cappuccino. Panel A is the steaming machine, panel B is the barista's hands removing the pitcher, panel C is when the hands clean the nozzle, and panel D is when the barista adds the dollop of foam. The camera never moved; only the action changed.

Background—Naming the background for this particular sequence could be as simple as "Café Interior" if only one background is to be used. But it is possible to have different backgrounds even within the same sequence. For example, the opening shot from within the café could show the baristas working the espresso machines in the background. If the woman storms out the door at the end of the sequence, we could show a street scene through the café window. Each background would be named accordingly, and that name would be indicated in the storyboard.

Action—Assist your visual by describing all that is happening within the panel. Be as descriptive as you need to be because this will help you "play the movie in your head" when it comes time to animate. In our café, example, you could describe the activity in the café. Is it a busy afternoon, or a quiet evening? Does the camera follow the coffee cup as it falls off the table? If so, do you

feature. Let's dissect a couple of animatics-in-progress to get an overview of how they were made.

FIGURE 6-4   Using rough sketches to determine movement in an animatic.

Open **Animatic_1.fla** in the enclosed DVD to see how simple keyframes were used to quickly ascertain movement of both the character and camera. From the top menu, go to **Control ▶ Play** to have the animatic play on its own. You can drag the red scrubber bar back and forth to replay any portion of the sequence as you wish. To view the animatic in a new window, go to **Control ▶ Test Movie** or press **Ctrl+Enter**, and the animatic will loop. Close the window when you're done.

Now let's open **Animatic_2.fla** to see how scenes can be separated and organized.

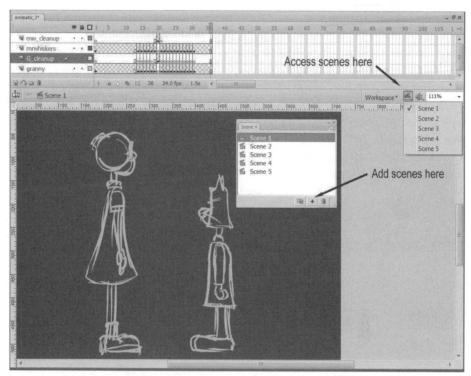

FIGURE 6-5   Using the **Scenes** feature in Adobe® Flash®.

When you first play the animatic from within the Adobe Flash file, you'll notice that it only plays 36 frames. Now press **Ctrl+Enter** on your keyboard to test the movie. You'll see that the animatic is significantly longer. The difference between this approach and that used to make the earlier file is that we have separated actions into scenes. Figure 6-5 shows you how to access each scene. By selecting a scene number, the Adobe Flash program will take you to that scene, allowing you to view it or edit it. You can add new scenes or delete unwanted scenes by going to **Window ▶ Other Panels ▶ Scene**. Click the **+** icon to add new scenes, select the scene you no longer want, and click the trash can icon to delete it. Double-click the scene name to rename it. The ability to rename your scenes can be very useful if you wish to stay consistent with the names you gave your sequences in your storyboards.

Now let's briefly look at an animatic with sound added to it. Open and play **Animatic_3.fla**. Looking inside the file, you'll notice that a waveform is visible along the timeline representing the imported audio. Above the waveform are notes sprinkled throughout, indicating what is being said. To make notes to yourself, create a new layer, move the scrubber bar where you want the note to begin, and press **F6** on your keyboard to make a blank keyframe. Click the blank keyframe once to select it, and type your comment in the **Properties** panel as indicated in Figure 6-6. Always precede your comment with two forward slash marks (///) for the Adobe Flash program to recognize it. When you've finished typing your comment, press **Enter** on your keyboard to submit it. The comment will appear on the timeline. You will find this feature very useful when you want to quickly make note of any gesture or camera movement you wish to match with a specific piece of dialogue, sound effect, or music.

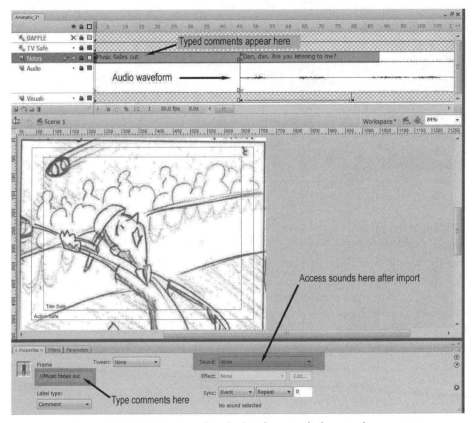

FIGURE 6-6   An animatic timed to match the sound.

TIMING IN ADOBE FLASH

Timing a scene in Adobe Flash is as easy as stretching out the keyframes on the timeline. Since we already know we are working with a file that is set to 30 frames per second, the only variable missing is the actual time as determined by our stopwatch. For instance, let's pretend that the amount of time it takes to get from the opening scene of the café, to the moment the cup hits the floor is 45 seconds. To determine the number of frames to place in your timeline for this sequence, you use this formula: 30 frames per second × 45 seconds = 1350 frames. Let's add some frames to a new Adobe Flash file now.

1. Open a new Adobe Flash file with the following settings: **Size** (720 × 540 pixels), **frame rate** (30 fps).
2. Our intent is to stretch the timeline to 1350 frames. To do so, drag the scroll bar at the bottom of the timeline all the way to the right, click just below a number on the timeline, and press **F5** on your keyboard. Flash will create one long blank keyframe. Repeat these steps until you have reached frame 1350.

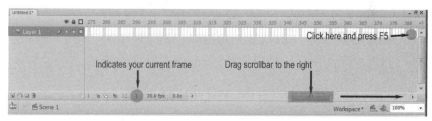

FIGURE 6-7   Drag the scrollbar to the end.

If you accidentally added too many frames, select the ones you wish to delete by dragging across the timeline and either pressing **Shift+F5** on your keyboard, or by right-clicking your mouse and selecting **Remove Frames**. See Figure 6-8. Once you have reached the desired number of frames, you can begin placing your drawings, audio, images, and anything else you need to make your film with the knowledge that it all must take place within your set timeframe.

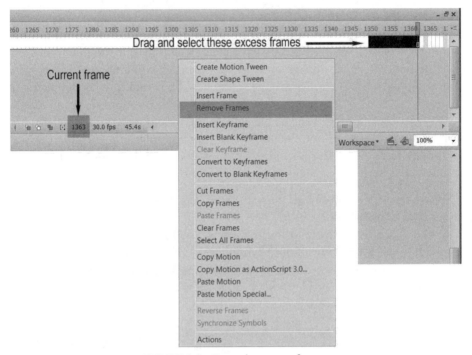

FIGURE 6-8   Removing excess frames.

CAMERA MOVEMENTS IN ADOBE FLASH

Several transitions and camera movements were covered in Chapter 4. Many can range in duration from a blink of an eye to a few seconds. Use the same formula mentioned previously to calculate longer camera movements, and use the next lessons to create the effects. Sample Adobe Flash files are located in the DVD for you to examine at your leisure.

Camera Cut

1. In this first lesson we're going to create the most common transition on television and film—the cut, a simple way to go from one scene to the next. When first opening a new file, be sure to use the default settings for both

the stage dimensions (720 × 540) and the frame rate (30 fps) as covered in Chapter 2.

2. Gather two images to represent your scenes and import them into a new Adobe Flash file by going to the top menu and choosing **File ▶ Import to Library**.

3. Open your Library (**Ctrl+L**) and drag the first image onto the stage. With the image selected, convert it to a symbol (**F8** on your keyboard).

4. Click **frame 60** on the timeline and press **F5** on your keyboard to extend the timeline. Your image will now be visible for two seconds.

5. Click **frame 61** on the timeline and press **F7** on your keyboard to create a new blank keyframe. Notice that your image has disappeared. Drag the red scrubber bar back and forth, and you'll see that your image is still visible for the first 60 frames. The second image will begin on **frame 61**.

6. Drag the second image onto the stage, convert it to a symbol, and click **frame 120** on the timeline. Again, press **F5** on your keyboard to extend the duration for which this second image will be visible.

7. That's all there is to it. Choose **Control ▶ Test Movie** from the top menu to see the outcome. Compare your result with the one provided (**Camera_Cut.fla**).

Camera Shake

1. When making the camera cut in the previous exercise, we created two keyframes and placed one image in each keyframe. To make a camera shake, we will use one image but several keyframes, and we'll move the image just enough to make it jump around.

2. In a new file, import a single image to the library and drag it onto the stage.

3. Click **frame 3** and press **F6** on your keyboard to create another keyframe. Do so again on **frames 5** and **7**. Each time you press **F6**, Adobe Flash will duplicate the previous frame and indicate it with a black dot. That black dot is your keyframe.

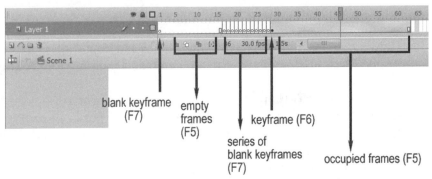

FIGURE 6-9   Distinguishing the different types of frames.

4. Select each keyframe and move the images in slightly different directions. Rotate them by pressing **Ctrl+Alt+S** on your keyboard. The **Scale and Rotate** pop-up panel will appear. Leave the **Scale** field as it is, and type −**2** for the rotation. Play with different degree settings, both positive and negative, to see the results.

5. Test the movie (**Control ▶ Test Movie**) to play the camera shake. Compare your results with the enclosed sample file **Camera_Shake.fla**.

FIGURE 6-10   The **Scale and Rotate** pop-up panel.

Camera Twist

1. Locate the file **Camera_Twist.fla** on the DVD, and test the movie to see what we will recreate next. This next example also uses keyframes, but to make the twist animate smoothly, we will use what Adobe Flash calls a Motion Tween. A Motion Tween is Adobe Flash's way of interpolating the animation between two keyframes. You will be responsible for the first and last positions of the image. Adobe Flash will do the rest.

2. Place an image in a new file, and convert it to a symbol.

3. Let the image occupy about 30 frames before animating the camera twist, and press **F6** on your keyboard to insert a new keyframe on **frame 31**. This new keyframe will be the first position.

4. Insert another keyframe at around **frame 45** and rotate it about 30 degrees. This is the second position of the twist. Drag the red scrubber bar back and forth to preview the effect. Next we will make the Motion Tween.

5. Click the first position (**keyframe 31**) and choose **Motion** from the **Tween** drop-down menu in the **Properties** panel. Another way to do this is to right-click your mouse and select **Create Motion Tween**.

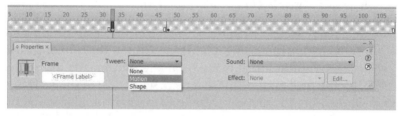

FIGURE 6-11 Creating a **Motion Tween** between two keyframes.

FIGURE 6-12 A **Motion Tween** applied.

6. Drag the red scrubber bar back and forth to see what we have so far. The movement is smooth, but it ends rather abruptly.

Traditional animators often apply what is called slo-in and slo-out to gently transition from a still position to motion and vice versa. In Adobe Flash this is called "ease in" and "ease out," and it is located in the **Properties** panel just below the **Tween** drop-down menu (you must have already selected **Motion** to make easing visible). One way to think about this principle is to pretend you are in your car resting at a traffic light. "Easing in" is when the light turns green and you first press the gas pedal to move forward, slowly gaining speed. "Easing out" is when you're driving along and the traffic light turns red, causing you to step on the brake until you come to a complete stop.

7. To complete the camera twist, select the first position keyframe, and drag the Ease slider all the way up to **100**, thus easing out of the Motion Tween. Test the movie to view your results. Just for comparison, drag the Ease slider all the way down to **−100** to ease in and test the movie again.

Rack Focus

1. So far, every camera effect has been accomplished on just one layer. For this next example, you will need two layers: a foreground layer and a background layer. Open the file **Camera_Rackfocus.fla** and test the movie to see the effect.
2. Create some foreground assets and a background image, and separate them onto their respective layers as indicated in the sample.fla.

As you've already seen in Chapter 5, when converting raw art to a symbol, you are given the option of making it a **Movie Clip**, a **Button**, or a **Graphic**. So far, choosing **Graphic** for simulating camera movements has sufficed. If you'll recall, for the final exercise in Chapter 5, we animated smoke rising from a chimney. Our reasons for choosing **Movie Clip** was twofold: first, because an animation nested within a movie clip will loop endlessly, even if the symbol is sitting on just one frame in the main scene. The second reason was that filters can only be applied to **Movie Clips**, not **Graphic** symbols. To create the rack focus effect, we will be applying the blur filter using the same steps as used to blur the smoke in Chapter 5.

3. Convert your foreground and background art into separate movie clips.
4. Insert keyframes for both layers on **frames 45** and **75**.
5. Lock the foreground layer and position the scrubber bar on **frame 45**. Select the background layer by clicking on its instance on the stage. Add a blur filter with a slider setting of **20**.
6. Right-click on the keyframe and add a **Motion Tween**.
7. From the **Properties** panel, apply an ease out of **100**.
8. Drag the scrubber bar to see the effect. Lock the background layer and unlock the foreground layer.
9. Position the scrubber bar on **frame 75**. Select the foreground layer by clicking on its instance on the stage. Add a blur filter with a slider setting of **20**.
10. Select the first position keyframe and add a **Motion Tween**.
11. Apply an **Ease Out** of **100**.
12. Drag the scrubber bar back and forth for a preview, and finally test the movie.

The Cross Dissolve

1. Open **Camera_crossdissolve.fla** to preview the effect. Again we will use two layers and two images, this time to fade from one scene to another.
2. Create two layers, place the first image on the top layer and convert it to a symbol. Duplicate the keyframe on **frames 45** and **70** (the cross-dissolve will take place between these two frames).
3. Create a blank keyframe at **frame 71** by pressing **F7** on your keyboard. Extend this blank keyframe several frames by pressing **F5** a few times.
4. Move the scrubber bar to **frame 70** and select the image on the stage. Locate the **Color** drop-down menu on the **Properties** panel, and choose **Alpha**. Use the slider to the right and move it all the way down to **0%** to make it invisible (this is similar to the Opacity slider in Photoshop®).
5. Click the keyframe on **frame 45**, create a **Motion Tween** and **Ease Out 100**. At this point the effect is complete. All that is needed is the second image beneath to be revealed.
6. Lock the top layer and insert a keyframe on **frame 45** of the bottom layer. Place the second image on the stage and have it occupy the same number of frames as the top layer. Line it up to match the image on the top layer. Test the movie.

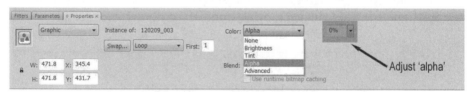

FIGURE 6-13   Adjust opacity of an image using its **Alpha** slider.

Fade to Black

1. The easiest method for fading a scene to black is to place an overlay on a layer above your scene and animate it from **0% alpha** to **solid black**. The key is to make the overlay a solid black rectangle and convert it to a symbol. Use the tools covered in the previous lessons to recreate the effect shown in the enclosed file **Camera_fadetoblack.fla**.

Truck In

1. In this next effect, the camera pushes in slowly to narrow the viewer's focus, so the movement should be slow and smooth. Test the movie from the file **Camera_TruckIn.fla**.
2. Create one layer, import an image onto the stage, and convert it to a symbol.
3. Duplicate the **keyframe (F6)** on **frames 40** and **155**.
4. Select the image on **keyframe 155** and press **Ctrl+Alt+S** to call up the **Scale and Rotate** window. Scale the image up about **150%** and click **OK**.
5. Create a **Motion Tween** between frames **40** and **155**.
6. Next, we want to have the camera start out a little faster and slow it down to a stop, in other words, Ease In to its motion and Ease Out of motion. To do this, create another keyframe in the middle of the **Motion Tween**.
7. Move the Ease slider down to −**40** for the first **Motion Tween** and **40** for the second.
8. Test the movie.

Pan Across

1. A camera panning across a scene is simply a Motion Tween between two keyframes with the image moving from left to right or vice versa.

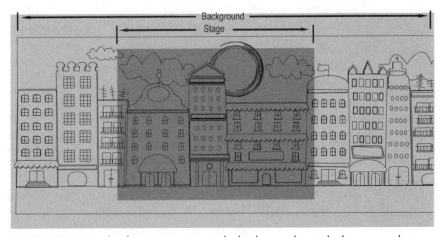

FIGURE 6-14   To simulate a camera pan, the background must be large enough to scroll across.

Pan Up

1. Panning up is exactly the same as panning across, except for the direction of movement. See the file **Camera_PanUp.fla** to see an example of panning different assets at different rates. Doing so creates what's known as the "parallax effect," which will be covered in the next example.

Parallax Effect

1. Open the file **Camera_Parallax.fla** and test the movie. This effect combines a pan across with added depth. As you might suspect, the depth is due to panning assets on different layers. By moving the assets in the foreground layers a greater distance left to right than those in the back layers, you achieve the effect.

2. Zoom out of the scene (**Ctrl+minus**) as far as possible to get a better sense of how far each symbol was moved in the enclosed file. Drag the scrubber bar to preview the animation.

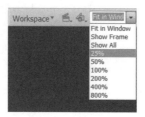

FIGURE 6-15 Zooming in or out of a scene.

Iris In/Out

1. For this example, we will explore the enclosed file **Camera_Iris.fla**. Test the movie to see the .swf play.

2. Unlock the bottom layer of the .fla and double-click on the symbol to go inside. The first things to note are the different types of layers. The top layer was converted from a **Normal** layer to a **Mask** layer. The middle layer was made into a **Masked** layer and the bottom layer was left as a **Normal** layer.

FIGURE 6-16 A **Mask** layer and a **Masked** layer work together and can be identified by their icons.

3. Ironically, the **Mask** layer actually reveals the layer beneath it. Preview each layer using the scrubber bar and hiding the other two layers to see what is happening.

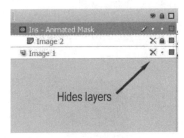

FIGURE 6-17 Click below the **eye** icon to hide a layer. Clicking the **eye** itself hides all layers.

4. You'll notice that the top **Mask** layer is the animated iris—a simple circle that was made into a symbol and scaled up and down. Figure 6-18 and Figure 6-19 show how to access a layer's properties for conversion.

FIGURE 6-18   Right-click on a layer to make it a **Mask** layer.

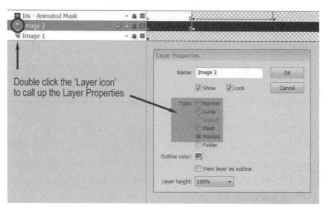

FIGURE 6-19   Double-click the layer's icon to bring up the **Layer Properties** panel.

5. The middle layer is what is being revealed, thus it is the **Masked** layer. To see the effect work, both layers must be locked.

Note: A mask can take any shape and works as a still image as well. It can be used to show a reflection in a mirror, a view through a window, a textured pattern through text, or a glimmer across something shiny.

Wipe

1. The camera wipe is another use of the mask feature in Flash. **Camera_ wipe.fla** takes the wipe a step further creatively by adding a motorcycle to lead the way. Hide the **Motorcycle** layer and scrub across the timeline, and you'll see that the wipe is just as effective, but not as fun. Let's see how this mask was made.

2. Zoom out as far as you can and lock and hide all of the layers except the **Mask** layer. Scrub across the timeline to see what the mask is doing.

3. As you can see, the mask is an irregular shape that has been made into a symbol and animated across the stage with a simple Motion Tween. Make the **Motorcycle** layer visible, scrub across the timeline again, and you'll see that the irregular shape of the mask was necessary to match the angle of the motorcycle and its rider.

4. Masks are fun because of their potential for creativity, and it can be tempting to make some very unusual camera wipes using masks. But remember that the wipe you choose should be consistent with the emotion of the two scenes it is tying together. You wouldn't want your wipe to overpower the scene and jolt the viewer.

SOUND

In Chapter 2, we learned that when recording dialogue, it's a good idea to leave some room before and after each recording to avoid accidentally cutting off a word. Having saved your dialogue as either .wav, .aif, or .mp3, you can import it into Adobe Flash in the following manner. Use your own sound clip or the one provided: **dourvoice.wav**.

1. Open a new file and go to **File ▶ Import ▶ Import to Library**. Locate a sound file and click **Open**. It will look like nothing happened, but open your Library, and you will see a sound file.

2. Click the sound file in the Library once, and a waveform will appear in the Library's preview pane.

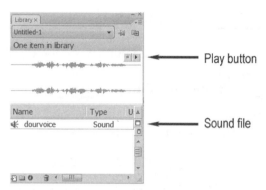

FIGURE 6-20 A sound file in the Library.

3. In the upper right corner of the preview pane, there is a **Play** button. Click it to preview the sound.
4. To place the sound on your timeline, click the blank keyframe and select the sound from the drop-down menu in the **Properties** panel.

FIGURE 6-21 Information for all sound files can be accessed here.

5. To view the sound on your timeline, extend your frames by pressing **F5** on your keyboard until the entire waveform is in full view. Choose **Control ▶ Play**, or slowly scrub across the timeline to preview the sound clip. There may be some silence at the beginning and/or end of the clip. We will edit it in the next exercise.

FIGURE 6-22 A sound clip in need of some editing.

SOUND EDITING IN ADOBE FLASH

Though limited in its sound-editing capabilities, Adobe Flash does offer some basic solutions that may be all you need. Let's trim some audio and add a fade to an existing bit of audio using the **Edit Envelope**.

1. Click anywhere on the timeline to select the audio. With the audio clip, click the **Edit** button in the **Properties** panel.

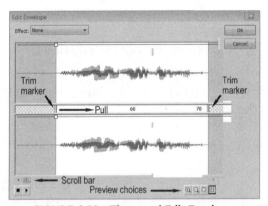

FIGURE 6-23   The sound **Edit Envelope**.

2. Pull the left trim marker to the right to remove the silence at the beginning.
3. Scroll all the way to the end of the clip and pull the right trim marker to the left, removing any silence at the end of the clip. Click **OK**.
4. The trimmed sound clip will show the adjustment on the timeline. Remove any excess frames from the timeline (**Shift+F5**).
5. Let's add a custom fade. With the sound clip selected, choose **Fade In** from the **Effect** drop-down menu in the **Properties** panel. Although it appears that nothing happened, when you open the edit envelope again you will see that the effect has indeed been applied. Test the movie to hear the new sound clip.

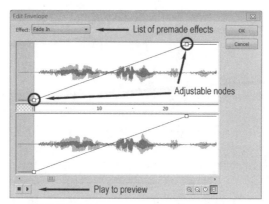

FIGURE 6-24   A pre-made effect applied.

SUMMARY

You have just taken a huge leap forward in the filmmaking process. With the material covered in this chapter, you can now translate your idea from text onto paper to a full-blown animatic with imagery, sound, and camera movement. In addition to covering the storyboarding process, we learned how to apply various rules of cinematography in Adobe Flash using the same tools and animation techniques used in professional animation studios. Once you have completed your storyboard, assembled all of your assets, and recorded your dialogue, you can begin creating your own animatic with the template provided on the enclosed DVD. Simply drag a copy of the **TV_template.fla** onto your desktop. Open the file and go to **File ▶ Save As**, and give it a different name to avoid overwriting the original file. In the next chapter, your characters will come alive through the magic of animation.

EXERCISES

Exercise 6.1

Rent your favorite movie and study the camera movements, timing, and transitions. Pause often throughout the film, and replay specific scenes while imagining how the story could be told differently using other camera movements.

Print out extra copies of the **Storyboard_Print.jpg**, and sketch out your solutions.

Exercise 6.2

Use a hand-held recorder to record ambient sounds from the world around you. Quite often, special effects sound more authentic when they are real. Examples of good ambient sounds include city traffic sounds, birds chirping in the park, a large group of people talking in a restaurant, subway trains, children playing in a school yard, and machines in a factory. Import these various sounds into a new Adobe Flash file, and layer them one on top of another to see what kinds of effects you get. Add a piece of music for even more richness.

Chapter 7 SHOW AND TELL

"Animation offers a medium of storytelling and visual entertainment which can bring pleasure and information to people of all ages everywhere in the world."

—Walt Disney

ANIMATION

An animator's task is to breathe life into a character in the same way that a puppeteer can pick up a lifeless doll and make it dance, laugh, or cry. What makes animation so special is that with just a few strokes of your pen, you can exaggerate a character's actions in ways no other medium can. For proof, pick up a copy of some classic Saturday morning cartoons and occasionally pause the DVD in mid-action. Even the greatest contortionists in the world couldn't pull off some of those moves.

When considering your character's actions, think of how your character would act in a given situation and why. Explore different possibilities, and remember: whenever possible, show, don't tell. If all your audience wanted was talking heads, they would simply flip on the evening news.

FIGURE 7-1   A smear can be used to add "snap" or blur to a movement. It is not so much seen as it is felt.

TWELVE PRINCIPLES OF ANIMATION

Just as you applied some simple drawing rules when designing your characters, you also have a dozen animation principles to guide you. Use them to show anything from how your character chews his food to how he runs away in fear. Aim for believability instead of realism, and your characters will be both convincing and entertaining.

1. **Squash and Stretch**—The act of deforming your character's shapes in order to give them weight and stress movement. When close up, the face should remain elastic, with each part reacting to another. When squashing or stretching your shapes, be sure they maintain their volume. Open the file **bouncingball.fla** for an example of how this principle is applied.

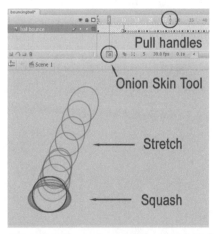

FIGURE 7-2   **Squash** and **stretch** revealed with the **Onion Skin Tool**.

2. **Anticipation**—A momentary reverse in action leading to the main action. It gives the audience a moment to prepare for a character's change in attitude or direction. Open the file **anticipation_mouse.fla** to see how the character momentarily leans back before taking off.

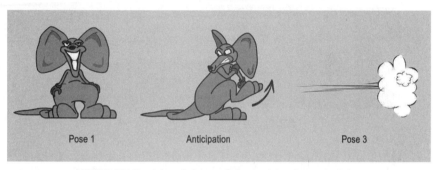

Pose 1   Anticipation   Pose 3

FIGURE 7-3   A breakdown of the Anticipation principle.

3. **Staging**—As mentioned in Chapter 5, a character's gestures should clearly reflect his/her attitude at any given time. If the facial expression is what is most important, move the camera forward. If body language is key, pull the camera back and experiment with different forward poses in silhouette.
4. **Straight Ahead vs. Pose-to-Pose**—When animating straight ahead, you begin with the first pose and work your way through the action frame by frame, with only a vague idea of how it will end. The unpredictability of this technique allows for improvisation and works best for wild gestures such as laughing uncontrollably or running around hysterically. With pose-to-pose animation, the key poses are first established and then in-betweened. This method is more controlled and is most effective with action that moves from one clear pose to another, such as a character raising a fork to his mouth, chewing his food, wiping his mouth, and then taking a drink. Most animations combine the two approaches to attain the desired effect.

FIGURE 7-4   Straight Ahead vs. Pose-to-Pose

5. **Drag and Follow-through**—While standing, keep your arm loose at your side and raise it above your head. Notice that your hand will drag slightly behind the rest of your arm and settle into position. This same effect can be seen when a girl with a ponytail turns her head, a person wearing a long coat is running and then comes to a complete stop, and a dog wags its tail. In other words, anything that is flexible will tend to drag until it stops and will then continue moving forward and overlap until it settles. See the file **dog_head_turn.fla** for an example of a dog's ears animated with overlapping action.

Ponytail settles into position.

FIGURE 7-5   Drag and Follow-through

6. **Slow-in and Slow-out**—This concept deals with how far apart you space your drawings. The closer they are, the slower the movement; the farther apart, the faster the action. In Adobe® Flash®, we have the ability to use "ease in" and "ease out." "Easing in" is the equivalent of sitting in your car

at a stop light and then lightly pressing the gas when the light turns green. Your car will ease into the movement. Assuming you've been driving along for awhile and then come upon a red light, you will then step on the brake and "ease out" of motion until you come to a complete stop. The purpose of this principle is to make motions more natural by varying the spacing of your drawings. If all of your drawings were evenly spaced, your animation would look very monotonous and lifeless—the exact opposite of what we're trying to achieve. See the file **motionguide_tween.fla** for the application of both easing in and easing out as a ball rolls down and up a hill.

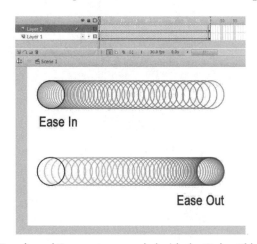

FIGURE 7-6   **Ease-in** and **Ease-out** as revealed with the **Onion Skin Tool** activated.

7. **Arcs**—When moving from point A to point B, things in nature rarely move in a straight line. Rather, they move in slight arcs. This includes the human body, whether it's a head turning from side to side or a hand pointing outward. Draw a path of action to use as a guide when establishing your key poses and follow that path when filling in the in-betweens.

FIGURE 7-7   The principle of arcs used with an arm coming forward.

8. **Secondary actions**—Rarely do things animate one at a time. To prevent your animations from looking robotic, you will want to include smaller secondary movements to support your main action. These secondary actions are meant to reinforce your intention, not detract from it. Open the file **horserun.fla** to see the secondary actions of a horse's ear and tail as it races across a track. Without these small details, the run would look stiff and mechanical, even at this rough stage.

FIGURE 7-8   Secondary actions to reinforce a run cycle.

9. **Timing**—A character's acting is directly related to how well you time it. It's important to visualize an action in your head before attempting to animate it. As you do, count how many seconds the action takes: "a thousand one, a thousand two . . ." Remember, we're animating at 30 frames per second, so a two-second count would occupy a total of 60 frames. If animating on "twos," each drawing occupies two frames on the timeline. This way of animating is standard among most productions.

FIGURE 7-9   A timeline showing an animation on twos.

10. **Exaggeration**—If all you wanted was to create realism, you would make your film live action. The beauty of animation is that you can exaggerate facial expressions and gestures in ways live action can't. Exaggeration is used to amplify an idea or mood. Use it to your advantage.

11. **Solid drawing**—This concept goes back to the principles discussed in Chapter 3. Give your characters volume and depth. And use simple shapes for ease of manipulation. The simpler your initial design, the fewer lines you'll have to animate in the long run.

FIGURE 7-10   The drawing on the left uses simple shapes and clean lines, making it much more "animatable" than the drawing on the right.

12. **Appeal**—This concept summarizes all aspects of the story: character development, design, drawing, and acting. The more deliberate you are with your creation, the more appealing your film will be.

WALK CYCLE

Considering that most of us learned to walk as toddlers, the act of walking may be something that we've taken for granted. The truth is, quite a bit can be interpreted about a person by the way they walk, and sometimes you can recognize a person you know from a distance simply by their walk cycle. Set aside some time to observe real people walking and try to determine how they are feeling. Is their pace slow and casual as if they are merely taking a stroll? Are their feet dragging along, suggesting they really don't want to go where they are headed? Perhaps their pace is brisk because they are in a hurry. Or they step lightly because they are happy. See the file named **walk_cycles_rough. fla** for samples of two walk cycles with very different attitudes.

ROUGH ANIMATION

It's tempting to get bogged down in the details when roughing out your animation, but remember that the goal at this stage is to achieve clarity. Work fast by keeping your strokes broad and drawings small, then preview the motion with the scrubber bar or testing the movie. The cleanup process will come after you've attained the gesture and movement you're looking for. Open up the file **turkey_run.fla** to see a turkey's run cycle in the process of being cleaned up.

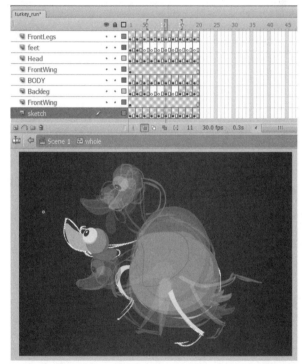

FIGURE 7-11   Use the **Onion Skin Tool** to preview drawings preceding and following your current frame.

When cleaning up your artwork, always draw it at 100% size *before* converting it to a symbol. This will ensure that you are not including minute details that won't be seen in the final film. It also maintains consistency across all duplicated instances of the original symbol. In other words, any scaling up or down should be done outside the symbol.

THE MOTION TWEEN WITH ROTATION

The Motion Tween is the single most popular method for animating in Adobe Flash. If you'll recall, we used it in Chapter 6 to create a camera twist. In this next exercise, let's apply some rotation to a Motion Tween to move the hands of a clock.

1. Open a new file and create three layers, one for the clock face, another for the hour hand, and a third for the minute hand.
2. Draw a circle for the clock face and convert it to a **Graphic Symbol**. Lock the layer.
3. In their respective layers, draw an hour hand and a minute hand. As you convert each into a symbol, notice that the registration points are in the center. We will change this in step 5.
4. Position the clock hands on the face.
5. Click the minute hand and select the **Free Transform Tool** from the toolbar (Shortcut key: **Q**).
6. With the **Snap to Objects** tool selected (the magnet icon on the toolbar), pull the registration point down to the center of the clock face so that the hand will rotate about its new axis. Do the same with the hour hand.
7. Insert keyframes (Shortcut key: **F6**) for both hand layers at **frame 60**. Extend the clock face out to **frame 60** as well (Shortcut key: **F5**).
8. Select the keyframes for the minute hand and hour hand on **frame 1** and right-click **Create Motion Tween**. You can also access the **Motion Tween** effect from the **Properties** panel.
9. We will now create the rotations for each hand, beginning with the minute hand. Click anywhere in the middle of the Tween and choose **CW** (clockwise) from the **Rotate** drop-down menu in the **Properties** panel. Then type **2** in the **times** input box.

FIGURE 7-12   The **Rotate** drop-down menu.

10. Repeat step 9 with the hour hand, but type **1** for the number of times it will rotate. That's all there is to it. Compare your results with the enclosed file **clock.fla**.

SHAPE TWEEN

Shape Tweens are used to create smooth, organic movements like an inflating balloon, or melting butter. Though Shape Tweens can be quite unpredictable, they're worth knowing about because when they do work, they're a great time saver. On the other hand, if you find yourself having trouble controlling a Shape Tween, switch over to drawing your animation frame by frame. Open **shapetween.fla** for an example of our next exercise.

1. In a new file, create a shape and do not convert it to a symbol. Unlike Motion Tweens, Shape Tweens must remain raw art in order to work.
2. Insert a keyframe at **frame 15** and alter the shape slightly (the more drastic the change, the more unpredictable the result). Continue to insert keyframes every 15 frames for a couple of seconds' worth of animation, altering the shape along the way.
3. Select each keyframe and right-click to select **Create Shape Tween**. If you prefer, choose **Shape** from the **Tween** drop-down menu in the **Properties** panel. A mint green color on the timeline will differentiate it from the lavender color of a typical Motion Tween. If you like, add easing in and easing out for a change of pace.
4. Test the movie to see your results. Experiment with different shapes for a variety of outcomes.

Refer to **shapetween_advanced.fla** for a more sophisticated use of the Shape Tween. Click the **ocean waves** symbol to see how the effect was created.

MOTION GUIDE

Motion guides serve as paths for your object to follow. Examples of their use include the path of a butterfly, the arc of a thrown ball, or the gentle falling of leaves. Let's make an animation of a mosquito flying in the shape of a figure eight. Refer to **motionguide_mosquito.fla**.

1. In a new file, draw a mosquito and convert it to a symbol. Move the edit point toward the mosquito's nose.
2. Add a keyframe on **frame 45**.
3. Right-click the mosquito layer and choose **Add Motion Guide**. A new layer will be placed above the mosquito layer, and the layer below will be indented.

Motion path ——————→

Makes layer invisible ——————→

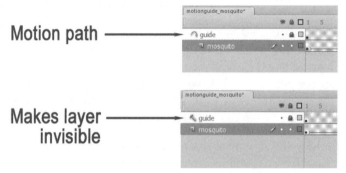

FIGURE 7-13   The difference between a **Motion Guide** layer and a **Guide** layer.

4. In the new **Motion Guide** layer, draw a figure eight with the pencil tool and smooth it out completely by clicking the **Smooth** tool in the toolbar multiple times. Create a small gap somewhere along the loop so that you have a starting point and an ending point along the shape.
5. In **frame 1**, snap the mosquito's edit point to the beginning of the loop.

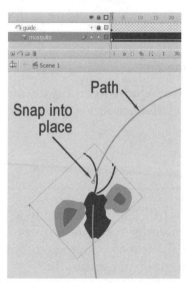

FIGURE 7-14   Snap each symbol to the two endpoints of the loop.

6. In **frame 45**, snap the mosquito's edit point to the end of the loop.
7. Click the first keyframe and create a Motion Tween.
8. Move the scrubber bar to see an update. From the **Properties** panel, check the **Orient to Path** box.
9. Test the movie to view the result.

Once again open the file **motionguide_tween.fla** to see how the ball's path was made using a motion guide and how rotation was applied to make the ball roll.

NESTING SYMBOLS

When animating in Adobe Flash, you will want to begin with the smaller details first, and then work your way out. For example, if your character speaks a line of dialogue, the process works like this:

1. Listen to the audio.
2. Visualize the acting and establish the timing.
3. Sketch out a rough animation with key poses.
4. Place your cleaned up character into position.
5. Animate the mouth and eyes to match the dialogue.
6. Outside the head symbol, animate the head, body, and limbs.
7. "Nest" the entire character's animation into one symbol so the entire animation is self-contained.

Let's "nest" a simple animation of a car animating across a screen. The file **car_nestedmc.fla** has been provided for reference.

1. In a new file, draw a wheel, convert it to a symbol, and animate it with a full rotation for 1 second.

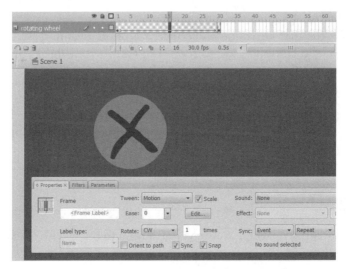

FIGURE 7-15   A clockwise-rotation Tween applied.

2. Now we will embed (nest) this animation within a symbol. Click on the layer, hover over the frames on the timeline, and select **Cut Frames**.

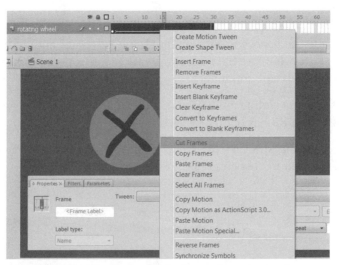

FIGURE 7-16   Cutting all the frames from the timeline.

3. Draw a rectangle on the stage. Convert it to a symbol and name it "**animated wheel**." Choose **Movie clip**. Click **OK**.

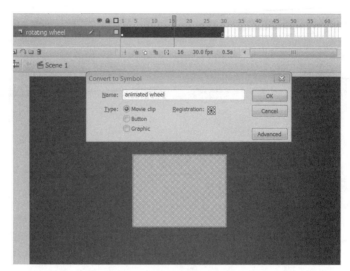

FIGURE 7-17   Using a rectangle as a temporary placeholder.

4. Open the **Align** panel (Shortcut key: **Ctrl-K**) or via **Window ▶ Align** and click the **To Stage:** icon. Then click **Align Horizontal Center** and **Align Vertical Center** to position the rectangle in the middle of the stage.

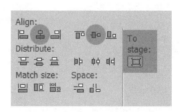

FIGURE 7-18   The **Align** panel.

5. Double-click the rectangle symbol to go inside the symbol. Right-click the keyframe and select **Paste Frames**. This pastes the animated wheel into the symbol, thus "nesting" the animation.

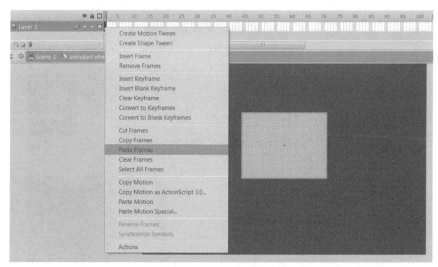

FIGURE 7-19 Pasting the frames into the rectangular placeholder.

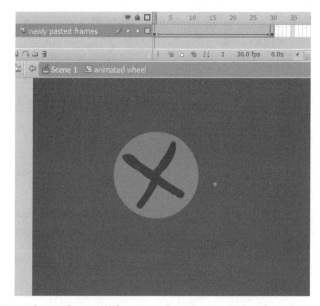

FIGURE 7-20 The newly pasted frames replace the rectangle. The animation is now nested.

6. Click **Scene 1** to go outside the symbol and duplicate the wheel by selecting it and pressing **Ctrl+C** (Copy) and **Shift+Ctrl+V** (Paste In Place). Move the duplicated wheel over to the left or right.

7. On another layer, draw the body of the car and convert it to a symbol.

8. Let's move the car across the stage. First, shift-select both layers, hover over the timeline, and right-click to choose **Cut Frames**.

9. Click a blank frame in one of the empty layers and repeat steps 3, 4, and 5. Assign a different name to the symbol. This nests the entire car inside a symbol.

10. Go outside the symbol and position the car all the way to the left of the stage on **frame 1** and insert a keyframe on **frame 30**. Position this new keyframe all the way to the right of the stage. Create a Motion Tween from **frame 1** to **30**. The car is now moving across the stage.

11. Cut the frames once more and paste them inside another symbol, just as we did earlier. This effectively places the entire car's animation inside one symbol. Assuming you made all of your symbols into movie clips, you can have the car occupy one frame on the main scene and still see the animation play in its entirety when you test the movie.

12. The other advantage to nesting animations is that you can duplicate the main symbol several times, scale each one up and down, and end up with a whole fleet of cars animating across your stage.

FIGURE 7-21   Still shots from the enclosed file **Nested_symbols.fla**.

For more advanced samples of how the techniques above can be applied, check the following files: **rotation.fla**, and **firefly.fla**.

ANIMATING DIALOGUE

When animating dialogue, you will temporarily add the audio into the character's head symbol. Once the mouths have been matched to the audio, be sure to cut and paste the audio onto the main timeline, so it can be heard when testing the movie. Refer to the enclosed DVD and play the recorded videos **Mouths_01**, **Mouths_02**, and **Mouths_03** to view step-by-step tutorials on animating dialogue. Figure 7-22 below is a typical mouth chart. The numbers in parentheses under the phonemes are the instance numbers you would input in the **Properties** panel to call out the specific phoneme as shown in the video **Mouths_02**.

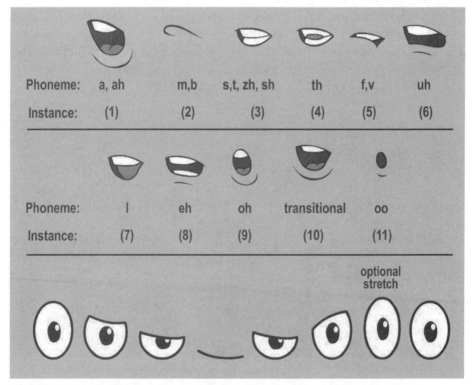

FIGURE 7-22   A basic set of mouths with their respective sounds along with a simple eye blink.

SPECIAL EFFECTS

Animation is a visual medium. Its strength lies in the power to create memorable images. When reviewing your script, look for situations where motion graphics may convey your message more effectively than dialogue. Here's an example. Suppose your character suddenly felt dizzy. An unimaginative solution would be to have your character say, "Uh, oh. I feel dizzy." The problem with this is that the viewer is removed from what the character is feeling. They see that something is wrong, but they don't feel it. A better solution would be to present the situation from within the character's head. Try envisioning the camera closing in on her eyes, and then turning toward the object she is looking at. The camera then blurs into a scene of frenzied shapes and squiggles moving about, just before revealing the character on the ground. Your audience has now participated in the event and not just been a bystander. Motion graphics are a great solution for creating stunning transitions, striking emotions, and dramatic atmosphere. See the file **specialeffects.fla** for ways to create cartoony speed lines, a smoke screen, a shiny glimmer, and a laser.

CREATIVE TITLE AND CREDITS DESIGN

Title sequences can be much more than simple white text on a black background. Many feature films cleverly incorporate gags, bloopers, or even mini-stories to keep the audience entertained as the credits roll by. Watch as many movie trailers online as possible to get ideas for your own credit sequence.

As for the titles themselves, let's see how we can make some eye-popping special effects using all that we've learned so far in combination with various movie-clip filters. Though the results look advanced, everything you see in these ten examples was completed using the techniques covered in Chapters 3, 5, 6, and 7. Feel free to review those chapters at any time during these lessons for a refresher course on the basics.

PROJECT 1: STEAMPUNK

Test the movie **Texteffect_steampunk.fla** to see the end result. The primary devices we will use are keyframing (Chapter 5), Motion Tween (Chapter 6), masking (Chapter 6), rotation (Chapter 7), nesting (Chapter 7), and gradients (Chapter 3).

1. In a new file, type the text you wish to design around. Typography design is an art in itself. Choose a font that conveys the feeling you wish to come across, in this case: mechanical, futuristic. We also need a font that has some girth to it, so we can fill it with our gears, clocks, screws, and metal plates.
2. Break apart the text, convert it to a movie clip, and give it a name. This movie clip will contain the entire animation that occurs inside the letters.
3. Add a thick 8-point stroke to the fill of the text with the **Ink Bottle** tool and cut (**Ctrl-X**) the fill.
4. Create a new layer and place the new layer below the text. **Paste in Place** (**Shift-Ctrl-V**) the fill. This fill will act as a mask. Go ahead and name the layer "mask."

FIGURE 7-23 The outline and fill separated into two layers.

5. Right-click the **mask** layer and choose **Mask** from the drop-down menu.

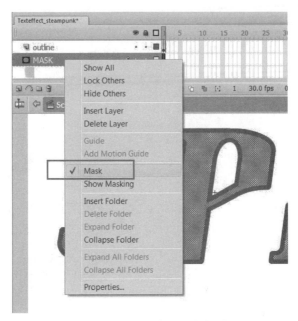

FIGURE 7-24   Creating the mask for the gears.

6. Lock both layers and create a third layer below the mask layer. Name it "**gears**," and right-click the layer. Choose **Properties. . .** and select **Masked**. Click **OK**.

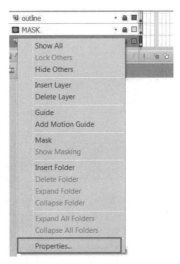

FIGURE 7-25   Assigning a layer's properties.

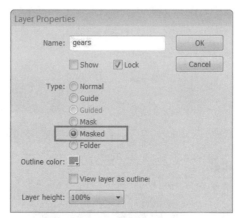

FIGURE 7-26   Making a **Masked** layer.

7. Let's make some gears and other moving parts. In this example, we have several gears rotating clockwise and counterclockwise, pistons pumping up and down and sideways, a clock's hands rotating at different speeds, and metal plates and screws sitting in one place.

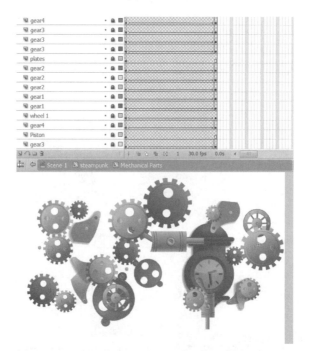

FIGURE 7-27   Every object is given its own layer to allow Motion Tweening.

8. Draw a perfect circle with the **Oval Tool** and convert it to a movie clip. As you draw the circle, hold down the **Alt-Shift** keys on your keyboard to keep it perfectly round, and start from its center. Gradients were applied to both fills and strokes as needed to get the best effect. See Figure 7-29 below for the exact settings used.

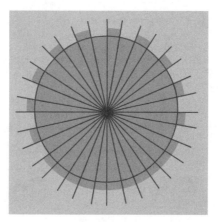

FIGURE 7-28   Constructing the gear with temporary construction lines.

FIGURE 7-29   The gradient settings used to create a gold metallic effect.

9. Once your first gear is complete, right-click it to duplicate the symbol. Give it a new name and change the gradient's settings to make it silver.

Duplicate the symbol a third time and make it copper. Then a fourth time to combine metals.

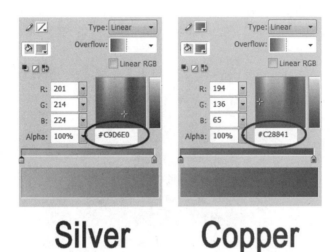

FIGURE 7-30 Gradient settings for silver and copper.

10. Now that you have four gears to work with, drag additional instances out of the library and onto the stage, and scale them up and down to create variety.
11. Arrange the gears around the stage. Select them and **Distribute to Layers**. Nesting all of the gears into one symbol will make moving them around as a group easier. If you haven't already done so, do that now.
12. Return to the mask and turn the mask on by locking both the **Mask** and **Masked** layers to check the placement of the gears.

FIGURE 7-31 Checking the arrangement of the gears within the letters.

13. Rotate some gears clockwise and others counterclockwise.

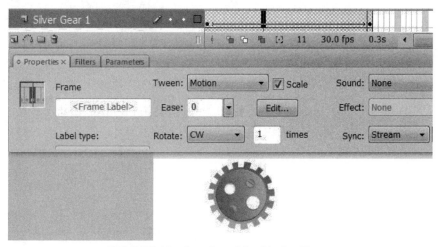

FIGURE 7-32 Rotating with a Motion Tween.

14. Now that you have your gears in motion, it's time to add some pistons. The piston is made up of two parts: the arm and the cylinder. The cylinder moves up and down on one layer, while the arm rotates back and forth on another.

To have the movement loop seamlessly, use three keyframes as shown in Figure 7-33, with the first and third keyframes being identical (starting and ending positions). Also note that the edit point on the arm has been moved up and to the left so that it can rotate about its new axis.

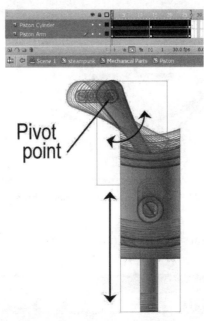

FIGURE 7-33 Rotating the piston's parts on individual layers. Movement shown via **Onion Skin Outlines.**

15. Add a second piston, rotate it 90°, and position both so that they too may be seen through the mask. Next up, the clock.

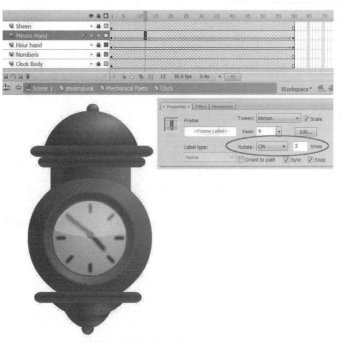

FIGURE 7-34   The clock in its entirety.

16. Notice in Figure 7-34 that the clock's parts have been separated into different layers. One reason for this is to make it easier for changes to be made on the fly. Take the sheen on the clock face, for example. The sheen was made by drawing a circle with a white fill, converting to a movie clip, and then setting its alpha (opacity) in the **Properties** panel to 50%. If you wanted to adjust the alpha to a different setting later on or reshape the sheen without affecting the drawings below it, you can, all because it's on its own layer.

17. To give the face some realism, the numbers on the clock were first converted to a movie clip to allow for a blur filter. The hands were each made into Movie Clips as well and had drop shadows applied through the **Filters** panel. See Figure 7-35 for their settings.

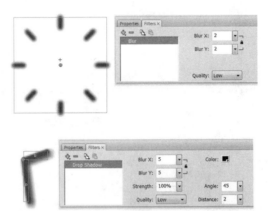

FIGURE 7-35 Filter settings for the numbers and hands.

18. The final step for the clock is to make the hands move. Figure 7-34 shows that the minute hand rotates two times clockwise every two seconds. To make the hour hand move more slowly, rotate it clockwise one time during the same two seconds. Just for fun, have one hand rotate counterclockwise and the clock will look like it's in desperate need of repair.

19. Check the placement of all your parts through the mask again, and continue to fill up any empty spaces as you see fit. Once that's done, go back to the main scene (Scene 1), and add a bevel to this entire movie clip. Feel free to experiment with your own settings, even adding glows and drop-shadows to see what you get. For this exercise, the settings shown in Figure 7-36 were what worked best.

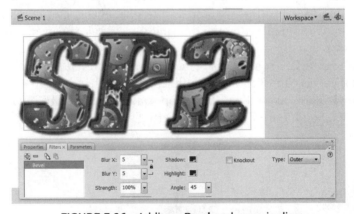

FIGURE 7-36 Adding a **Bevel** to the movie clip.

20. That takes care of the main title, but what this really needs is some atmosphere. To give it an old-time theater effect, we need to add film grain, scratches, a light flicker, spot light, and a dirty yellow film over the top. As you might have already guessed, the animated loops were made from movie clips. Figure 7-37 shows the individual layers used.

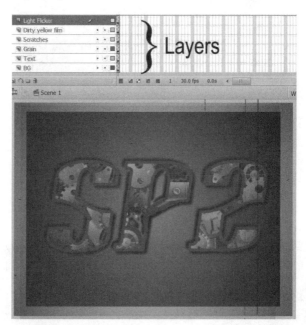

FIGURE 7-37   Layering the old-time film effects.

21. Let's begin with the light flicker. As Figure 7-38 shows, the flicker animation was made by scaling a radial gradient up and down and Shape Tweening it. The scaling of the gradient was accomplished via the **Gradient Transform Tool** (See Figure 7-39).

FIGURE 7-38 Gradients can be Shape Tweened.

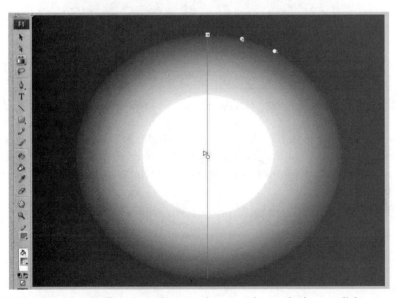

FIGURE 7-39 The **Gradient Transform Tool** was used to scale the spot light up and down.

22. The yellow film was also made with a radial gradient, but using a dark yellowish red instead of a charcoal gray.
23. The vertical scratch lines were made by drawing vertical lines with the line tool, breaking them apart and erasing parts of the fills. They were then converted into a movie clip and animated from side to side, occasionally disappearing by entering a blank keyframe. See Figure 7-40 for a detailed view.

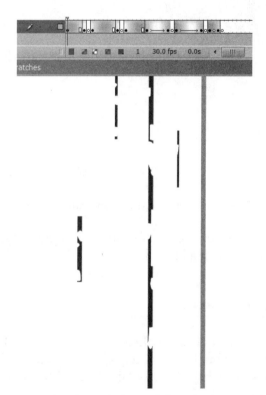

FIGURE 7-40   The vertical scratch lines Motion Tweened.

24. To make the film grain jump around in a frenzy, draw several tiny lines and shapes on the stage, duplicate the keyframes, and then flip them around vertically and horizontally. See Figure 7-41 below.

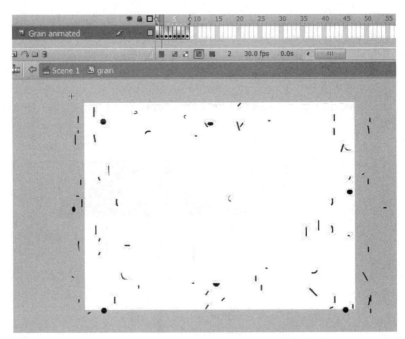

FIGURE 7-41   Keyframe animation of the film grain.

25. Lastly, we add a dark charcoal-colored gradient for the background to the bottom layer to tie it all together.

PROJECT 2: 70'S DISCO

Test the movie **Texteffect_shiny.fla** to see the end result. The primary devices we will use are Motion Tween (Chapter 6), masking (Chapter 6), rotation (Chapter 7), nesting (Chapter 7), and gradients (Chapter 3).

1. In a new file, create a total of four layers. Choose a retro-style font and type a simple piece of text on the bottom layer. Break it apart and fill it with a yellow color.

2. **Copy** this text and use **Paste in Place** to place it on the layer above it. Repeat this step until all four layers have a copy of the text. Name each layer as indicated in Figure 7-42.

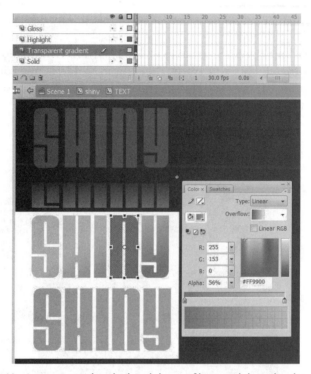

FIGURE 7-42   Layers named and a breakdown of how each layer has been affected.

3. Shift-select all of the frames and convert them into a movie clip. Go inside the movie clip to make the following adjustments.
4. To create the gloss effect on the top layer, fill the text with a solid white fill and set the alpha to 25%. Lock this layer when you're done.
5. To create the highlight, fill the text with a linear gradient running vertically with 100% white at the bottom and 0% white at the top. Chop off the bottom half of the text. Lock this layer when you're done.
6. For the transparent gradient, run a linear gradient diagonally from bottom right to top left using the settings shown in Figure 7-42.
7. Leave the bottom layer called "**Solid**" the original yellow. The text itself is complete. Now for the animated effects.
8. Test the movie and you will see a glint or sheen animate across the letters, some pink sparkles, and a reflection on the ground. Like the Steampunk example, the sheen is contained within the letters, which means we will rely on the magic of masking.

9. Create two layers, one mask and one masked. The mask layer will contain a copy of the text broken apart. The masked layer contains a couple of diagonal linear gradients that have been converted into a movie clip to allow for a horizontal Motion Tween (See Figure 7-43). When you've completed the animation, shift-select both layers and convert them to a movie clip so that it will loop when the movie is tested.

FIGURE 7-43   The animated sheen moving across the letters.

10. The sparkle began as some crisscross lines forming a star converted into a movie clip. This movie clip was then rotated counterclockwise and clockwise with easing applied from the first keyframe to the second. See Figure 7-44.

FIGURE 7-44   Initial setup of the sparkle.

11. The rotation animation is nested in a movie clip and a glow is applied. Figure 7-45 indicates the settings used. After the glow has been added, insert a couple of keyframes to animate the alpha of the sparkle appearing and disappearing. Duplicate these frames on separate layers and position the sparkle animations around the stage by clicking on the **Edit Multiple Frames** icon and stretching the scrubber bar's handles (Figure 7-46).

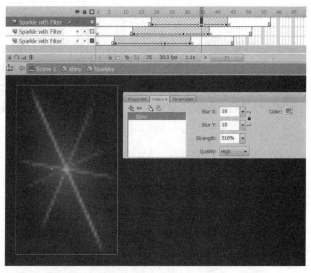

FIGURE 7-45   Adding a glow to the sparkle.

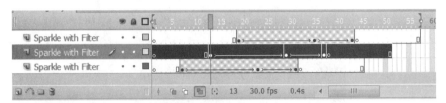

FIGURE 7-46 The **Edit Multiple Frames Tool** is used to move several frames of an animation at once.

12. The effect is almost complete. All that's left is the reflection on the ground. This is accomplished with two layers beneath the text layer. The bottom layer is simply a duplicate of the text layer flipped vertically, moved down on the stage, and assigned a 30% alpha. The middle layer is a linear gradient of deep purple from 100% alpha to 0% alpha. This gives the illusion that the reflection is fading away. Figure 7-47 shows the before and after effect of adding the middle layer.

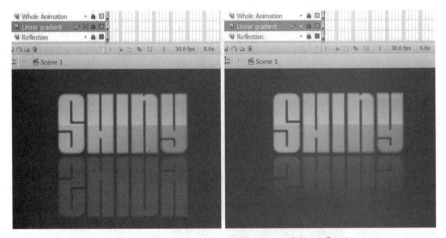

FIGURE 7-47 Side-by-side comparison of the reflection.

PROJECT 3: NEON GLOW

Test the movie **Texteffect_neonglow.fla** to see the end result. The primary devices we will use are Shape Tween (Chapter 7), keyframing (Chapter 5), gradients (Chapter 3), and Motion Tween (Chapter 6).

1. In a new file, create two layers. The top layer will contain the animation of the neon sign nested within a movie clip. The bottom layer will contain the animated lighting effect nested within its movie clip. The lighting on the wall will react to the animation of the sign, so let's create the letters first.

2. Figure 7-48 shows each letter with its own layer to allow for individual animation. The letters are given an icy blue gradient that is manipulated with the **Gradient Transform Tool**. The goal is to make the individual letters blink randomly. This is done by combining keyframe animation and Motion Tweening. Offsetting the animations by a few frames adds to the effect.

FIGURE 7-48   Creating a random animation for the letters.

3. With the animation complete, return to the main scene and apply the following filters: **Glow**, **Blur**, and **Drop Shadow**. The individual settings are shown in Figure 7-49.

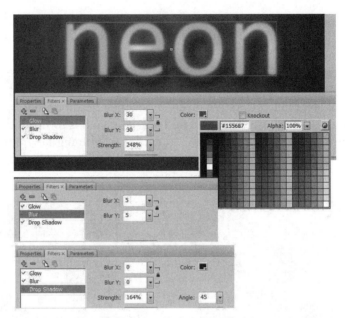

FIGURE 7-49 Settings applied to the neon-sign Movie Clip.

4. Okay, the neon sign is complete. Now the background layer in Scene 1 needs to be animated to reflect the glow of the sign. Animating the background is simply a Shape Tween of a radial gradient combined with some keyframe animation. See Figure 7-39 in the Steampunk example to see how the **Gradient Transform Tool** was used to increase and decrease the size of the radius. The logic behind the animation is that when a letter's light turns off, the radius of the glow in the background becomes smaller. Figure 7-50 shows the colors used for the gradient.

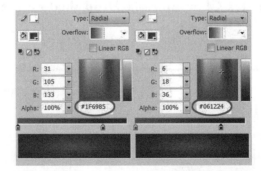

FIGURE 7-50 Settings applied to the background glow.

PROJECT 4: FREEZING ICE

Test the movie **Texteffect_freezing.fla** to see the end result. The primary devices we will use are alpha/opacity (Chapter 6), filters (Chapter 5), keyframe animation (Chapter 5), and gradients (Chapter 3).

1. In a new file, set the background color of your stage to a deep blue to contrast with the icy blue color of the ice block.
2. Create at least three layers, one for the text, a second for placing something behind the ice block to show through the ice, and a bottom layer for a linear gradient to add atmosphere.

FIGURE 7-51   The finished file.

3. Using a wide, chunky font, type the word you would like to use, convert it to a movie clip, break apart the text, and distribute each letter to its own layer.

snow			
edges			
cracks			
i			
c			
e			

Scene 1   ice

FIGURE 7-52   The text movie clip and its layers.

4. To make the letters look as though they're made of ice, each letter has a radial gradient that has been adjusted using the **Gradient Transform Tool**. The settings, from the center point outward, can be seen in Figure 7-53.

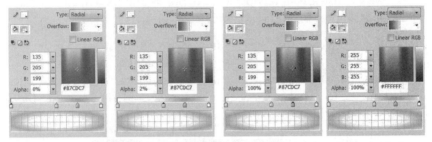

FIGURE 7-53   Radial settings for each letter to create a transparent, icy feel.

5. To create the "freezing" effect of each letter, the radius of the gradient is made smaller to give the appearance that it is solidifying. This is done by scaling the gradient down, again using the **Gradient Transform Tool**. Repeat this step for all of your letters. The animation may take about 85 frames and is achieved with a Shape Tween that eases out 100.

6. Above the letters, create another layer and create a movie clip to contain the animated cracks. The simplest way to animate these is to work backwards. Imagine how long it will take for the cracks to fill (in this case about ten frames). In the final frame, draw the cracks in full. Then insert a keyframe before the final frame and erase a small piece from each crack. Continue you to work in reverse, inserting a keyframe and erasing bits of each line until you arrive at the first frame, which will be empty.

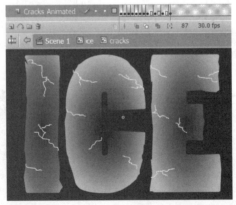

FIGURE 7-54   The cracks animated via keyframes.

7. To make the cracks look more authentic, some filter effects were applied: **Blur** and **Bevel**. See Figure 7-55.

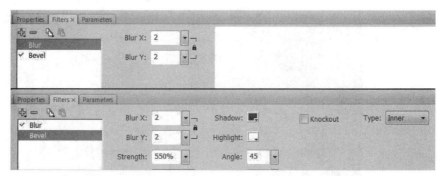

FIGURE 7-55   Filter effects applied to the animated cracks.

8. Next, add some icy edges to each letter by either using a white paintbrush or first outlining the edges with the **Pencil** tool and then filling it in with white. Convert this to a movie clip and then apply a **Blur** filter set to 5.

FIGURE 7-56   **Blur** filter applied to the icy edges.

9. Now for the fun part: making snow! On a layer above everything you've made so far, use a white paintbrush to paint some snow on the letters.

Convert this to a movie clip, and apply a **Bevel** and **Drop Shadow** with the settings provided below. Just like that, you have snow.

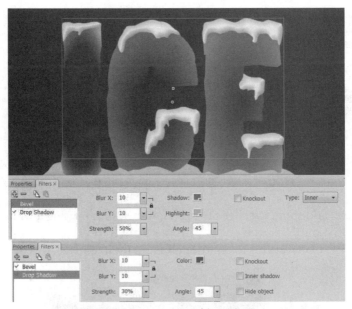

FIGURE 7-57 How to turn white paint into snow.

10. The snow on the ground is a tad more complex. Inside a separate movie clip, there are two layers: the top layer is a white glow that sits above an icy blue fill. The white glow was made by applying a blur setting of 37. The icy blue color can be created by typing **#87CDC7** next to the color swatch.

11. To complete the snow mound, apply the settings in Figure 7-58 to the entire movie clip.

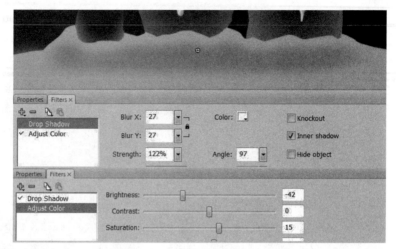

FIGURE 7-58 **Drop Shadow** and **Adjust Color** applied to the snow-mound movie clip.

12. Your final step is to return to the main scene and draw something behind the ice block to show that it is transparent. Add a linear gradient that runs vertically to create some nighttime atmosphere, and you're done.

PROJECT 5: MOVING LIGHT

Test the movie **Texteffect_lights.fla** to see the end result. The primary devices we will use are Shape Tween (Chapter 7), filters (Chapter 5), gradients (Chapter 3), and Motion Tween (Chapter 6).

1. The key to making this effect look realistic is to have the word's drop shadow react to the angle of the spotlight. In a new file, create a move clip that contains two layers. The top layer will contain the word, and the bottom layer will contain the background.

2. After typing the word, break it apart and apply a linear gradient that has a definite light source. In this example, the light source is located in the top left. Convert the word to a movie clip.

3. To further emphasize the direction of the light source, apply a **Drop Shadow** filter on the first frame with the angle set to 21. See Figure 7-59 for additional settings. At **frame 30**, insert a keyframe and change the angle of the drop shadow to 54. Motion Tween these two keyframes and

play the animation to see the drop shadow move. Add an easing out of 100 for a smooth arrival.

FIGURE 7-59   **Drop Shadow** settings for the text movie clip.

4. We want the animation to loop seamlessly, so select all of the keyframes, copy and paste them beginning on **frame 31**, and then right-click these new frames and select **Reverse Frames**. The animation will now return to the beginning.

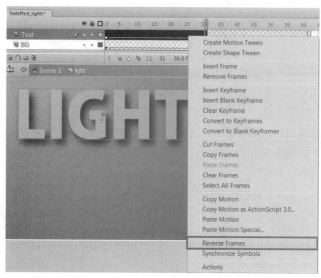

FIGURE 7-60   **Reverse Frames** to loop an animation back to the beginning.

5. Now the spot light. Figure 7-61 shows the settings to create the radial gradient for the background. To animate this gradient, insert a keyframe on **frame 30** and pour the paint bucket elsewhere. Return to the first keyframe and create a Shape Tween with an easing out of 100. Test your movie and adjust the location of the spotlight as necessary to react to your words' drop shadow.

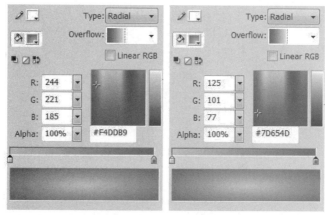

FIGURE 7-61   Radial gradient settings for a spotlight in the background.

6. If you're happy with the animation, duplicate and reverse the keyframes to the background's animation just like you did with the word's drop shadow in step 4.

PROJECT 6: DOWN IN FLAMES

Test the movie **Texteffect_fire.fla** to see the end result. The primary devices we will use are masking (Chapter 6), keyframing (Chapter 5), Onion Skin (Chapter 7), and Motion Tween (Chapter 6).

1. This example has several animations in it: flames burning, text cards disappearing, glow on the letters, red background vanishing, glowing embers and ash, and thin plumes of smoke. As you can imagine, the secret to making this work is the timing. Rather than trying to recreate this exact same sample, we are going to focus on creating each individual animation. This way, you can decide how you want to apply these techniques in your animations.
2. Open a new file set to 30 frames per second. Let's begin with the animating flames.
3. Within a new movie clip, draw several keyframes of fire burning using the **Onion Skin Tool** to see the prior frame. This example uses a combination of red, yellow, and white for each flame.

FIGURE 7-62   Keyframing the burning flames.

4. After completing the animation, add a glow with a yellow fill of **#FFCC33** and a **Blur** with the settings indicated in Figure 7-63.

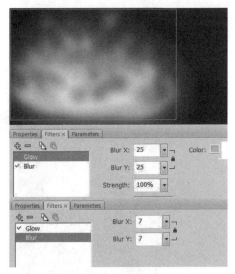

FIGURE 7-63   Glow and blur applied to the flames movie clip.

5. The letter cards were made by punching out the letters from rectangles with radial gradients applied. The gradients were then scaled up and down and Shape Tweened every couple of frames.

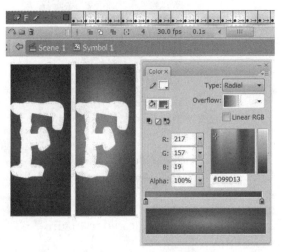

FIGURE 7-64   Shape Tweening the glowing effect on the cards.

6. As the glowing occurs, the cards slowly disintegrate. For each letter, add a **Mask** layer above the glow, and create a movie clip of a rectangle with its edit point at the bottom.

7. Motion Tween the rectangle animating downward as shown in Figure 7-65.

FIGURE 7-65 Motion Tweening the mask to make the card disintegrate. As the mask revealing the card moves down, the card vanishes.

8. Motion Tween the flame movie clip downward to follow the mask, and the burning card effect is complete.

9. Return to the main scene and apply a **Drop Shadow** filter to the entire movie clip. See Figure 7-66 for the settings.

FIGURE 7-66 **Drop Shadow** settings on the main movie clip.

10. Let's move on to the glowing embers. Like the flames, these too are keyframed with each frame alternating between yellow, orange, and red embers.

FIGURE 7-67   Keyframing the glowing embers.

11. After converting the glowing embers into a movie clip, apply a **Blur** and **Glow** filter as shown below to make it look like ash.

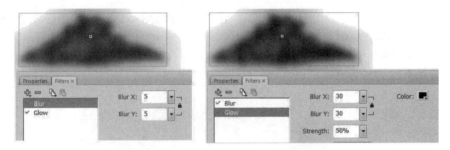

FIGURE 7-68   Filter settings for the ash.

12. Now for the smoke trails. To add variety, each trail movie clip is made up of three layers. Each layer contains an "S"-shaped curve that is Shape Tweened up and elongated along the way. The first keyframe is a gray fill with a 50% alpha, the second keyframe is the same gray set at 100% alpha, and the final keyframe is set to 0% alpha to make the trail disappear.

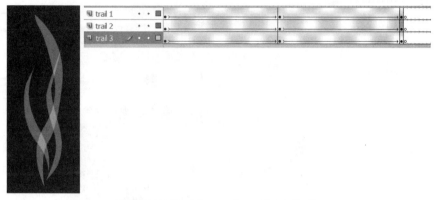

FIGURE 7-69   The smoke-trail movie clip.

13. The movie clips are then altered with **Blur** and **Glow** filters.

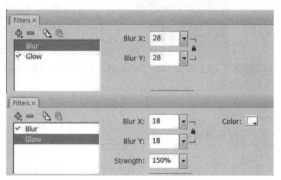

FIGURE 7-70   Filters used to finalize the smoke trails.

14. The final step is to make the shadow on the wall animate downward as well. This adds depth to the animation and helps add to the realism. In the main scene, create a movie clip, and fill it with a linear gradient as shown below. Keyframe animated flames, and return to the main scene to apply a **Blur** filter of 12.

FIGURE 7-71   **Blur** filter on the background animated movie clip.

PROJECT 7: LIGHT BURST

Test the movie **Texteffect_lightburst.fla** to see the end result. The primary devices we will use are motion guides (Chapter 7), gradients (Chapter 3), and Motion Tween (Chapter 6).

1. This example shows the movement of a spotlight similar to that which you would find coming from a lighthouse. Figure 7-72 illustrates the different keyframes involved.

FIGURE 7-72   The animated spotlight.

2. We'll begin with the actual spotlight. As you can see in Figure 7-73, the light follows a motion guide in the shape of a thin ellipse. As the spotlight moves along the guide, it changes scale. In a new file, draw an ellipse as shown in Figure 7-74.

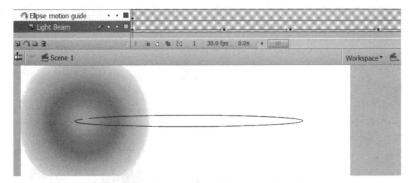

FIGURE 7-73   The spotlight's motion guide.

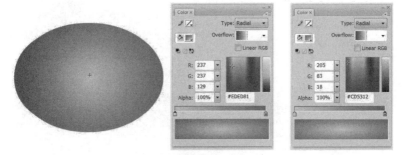

FIGURE 7-74   The ellipse and its radial gradient settings.

3. Place **Glow**, **Blur**, and **Gradient Glow** filters to the movie clip.

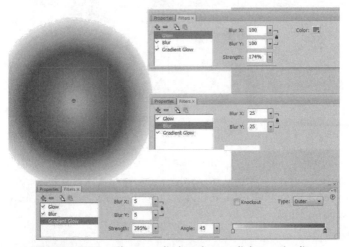

FIGURE 7-75   Filters applied to the spotlight movie clip.

4. As the spotlight moves back in "3D" space, it's darkened to give the illusion that it is farther away.

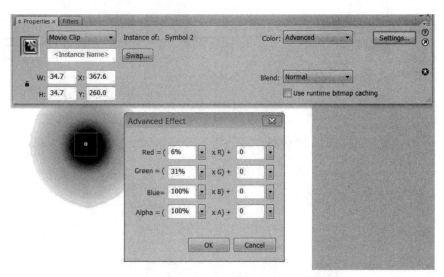

FIGURE 7-76 Lowering the brightness of the spotlight as it moves away.

5. Motion Tween the keyframes to animate the light around the elliptical motion guide. Be sure to snap the spotlight's edit point to the endpoints of the ellipse.

6. Now for the text. Type your text with a black fill and convert it into a movie clip. Each keyframe has a **Glow** and **Bevel** filter applied. The different settings for each keyframe are shown in Figure 7-77.

FIGURE 7-77   Both the **Glow** and **Blur** filters have different strengths depending upon the keyframe.

PROJECT 8: MASK REVEAL

Test the movie **Texteffect_RevealMask.fla** to see the end result. The primary devices we will use are Shape Tween (Chapter 7), masking (Chapter 6), filters (Chapter 5), and shape hints (new feature).

1. When you first open the sample file, it looks as if there is nothing on the stage. The keyframe on the timeline, however, assures us that there is indeed something there. Click on the keyframe in the timeline to highlight

the movie clip onstage. A small dot will appear in-stage. Double-click it to go inside the movie clip. Figure 7-78 shows what you will find.

FIGURE 7-78   Inside the main movie clip.

2. Let's recreate the effect now. In a new file, create a movie clip to contain the animation. You can do this by going to **Insert ▶ New Symbol**, giving the symbol a name, and clicking **OK**. You are now inside the symbol.
3. Create two layers, one to contain the large "S" or other curvy element, and another layer above to contain an animated mask. The mask will reveal the drawing or text below it. Figure 7-79 gives you a preview of how the mask animates down the timeline, slowly revealing the letter underneath.

> **TIP**
> To preview a mask at work, both layers must be locked.

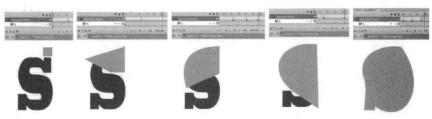

FIGURE 7-79   Animating a mask.

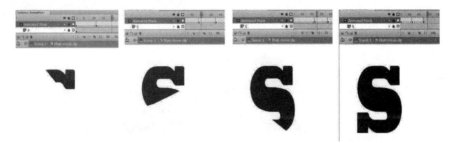

FIGURE 7-80   Lock both layers to view the reveal at work.

4. Break apart your letter/text. Convert the top layer to a **Mask** and make the bottom layer **Masked**.

5. As in the example, draw a small square or circle slightly away from the object you will reveal. Make sure you draw it in the **Mask** layer. This shape is what you will be sculpting as you move down the timeline. As stated earlier in the chapter, masks can be quite unpredictable. To help us control how the mask moves from one keyframe to the next, we will use **Shape Hints**. They don't always work, but when they do, the results are fun.

6. Imagine how long you want the animation to last from beginning to end. In this case, it lasts about one and half seconds, so a new keyframe is placed approximately every ten frames. It's not an exact science, so the number of keyframes may vary. The good news is that you can drag the keyframes back and forth along the timeline to work out the timing without affecting how the Shape Tween looks. Remember, the closer two keyframes are to each other, the quicker the movement. To slow an animation down, move the keyframes farther apart.

7. Lock the bottom **Masked** layer. At about **frame 10** of your top layer, insert another keyframe.

8. Pull the ends of your square to begin "revealing" your text. Refer back to Figure 7-79 as necessary.

9. Continue to pull and shape your mask around your letter as you move down the timeline. Figure 7-81 shows the right and wrong way to adjust your mask.

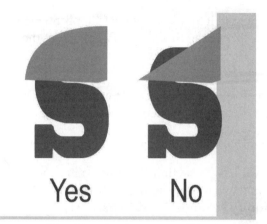

FIGURE 7-81   Any part of the object that is not covered by the mask will not be revealed.

10. Now that you've completely covered the text, it's time to apply the Shape Tween from one keyframe to the next.

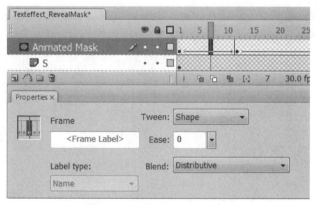

FIGURE 7-82   Applying a Shape Tween.

11. As you apply your Shape Tween, use the red scrubber bar to preview how the shape animates over the letter. Chances are, your Tween will become more unpredictable as it tries to curve around your shape. That's where Shape Hints come in.

12. Shape Hints are used for two things. They can either be used to tell two points to stay where they are, or they can be used to tell a point where you want it to go. Find a point in your animation where the mask is not acting

the way you want it to. We are going to apply Shape Hints on two keyframes in the hope of getting this Shape Tween to act the way we want it to.

TIP

If your Shape Tween simply does not want to cooperate after everything we're about to do, you may need to keyframe that particular sequence of frames.

---

13. Okay, so we have a section that's not behaving the way we want. Select the keyframe where the animation begins (we'll call it keyframe "a") and select **Modify ▶ Shape ▶ Add Shape Hint** from the top menu bar. See Figure 7-83.

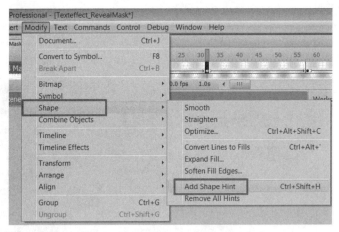

FIGURE 7-83 Creating a Shape Hint.

14. A little red circle with an "a" inside it will appear on the stage. This is your Shape Hint. Select and drag the Shape Hint toward the corner you wish to manipulate. Snap it into place.

TIP

Shape Hints work best when snapped into corners.

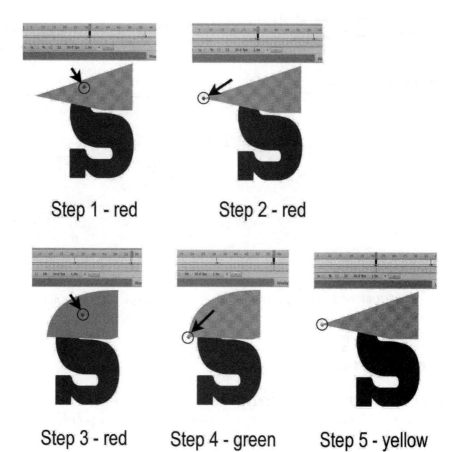

Step 1 - red   **Step 2 - red**

Step 3 - red   **Step 4 - green**   **Step 5 - yellow**

FIGURE 7-84   Step-by-step breakdown of applying Shape Hints.

15. Move to the next keyframe and add another Shape Hint. Snap this to where you want the point to end up. The Shape Hint will turn green when it has been snapped into place properly.

16. Go back to the first keyframe, and you will see that it has turned yellow. This confirms that both Shape Hints have been snapped into place.

17. After following the steps illustrated above, scrub across the timeline with the red scrubber bar to see if the mask is animating properly. If so, move on to another portion that could use the assistance of a couple of Shape Hints. Remember, Shape Hints can be used to tell a corner to stay in place, or to tell it where you want it to go.

18. Once the mask animation is complete, it's time to apply a couple of filters to the main movie clip in Scene 1 to get the dimensional effect you see in the example.

19. Figure 7-85 shows the settings used to create a bevel and drop shadow. Add these and you're done.

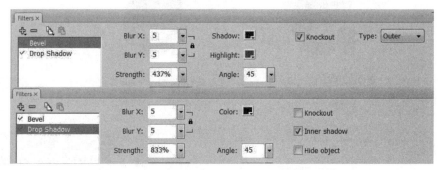

FIGURE 7-85   **Bevel** and **Drop Shadow** settings applied to the main movie clip.

PROJECT 9: ELECTRICITY

Test the movie **Texteffect_electricity.fla** to see the end result. The primary devices we will use are keyframing (Chapter 5), nesting (Chapter 7), and filters (Chapter 5).

1. When generating electricity, you want to make everything jitter: the background, the letters, and the electric charge. Let's begin with the background. In a new file, create three layers.

FIGURE 7-86   The three layers that make up the electricity file.

2. The background layer is a movie clip containing three keyframes, each with the center point of a radial gradient positioned in different places on the stage. This gives the illusion that the lighting on the wall is being affected by the glow of the electric current on the letters.

3. Moving on to the middle layer, type a simple word using a font with some thickness. Break apart the text and convert it to a movie clip. Within the movie clip, insert a few keyframes and reposition each letter just slightly so that they, too, jitter as if receiving an electric shock.

4. Outside this movie clip assign a **Glow**, **Bevel**, and **Blur** using the settings shown below.

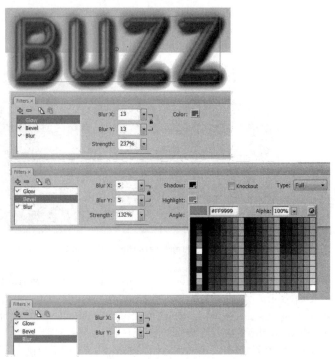

FIGURE 7-87   Filter settings applied to the text movie clip.

5. Now for the best part—making the electricity. The most important thing to know about how electricity moves is that no matter how manic the activity, the two endpoints typically remain in the same place. This example uses five keyframes to animate several bolts. Figure 7-88 shows the animation with the **Onion Skin Tool** selected. Use it as you draw each frame to make lining up the endpoints easier.

FIGURE 7-88 The **Onion Skin Tool** showing the five frames used to animate the bolts of electricity.

6. The last step is to apply the filters that will make the bolts glow with energy. See Figure 7-89 for the settings used.

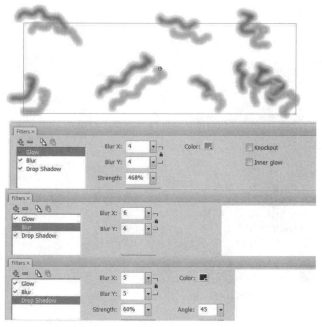

FIGURE 7-89 **Glow, Blur,** and **Drop Shadow** filter settings for the bolts.

PROJECT 10: MELTING BLOB

Test the movie **Texteffect_blob.fla** to see the end result. The primary devices we will use are keyframing (Chapter 5), nesting (Chapter 7), Onion Skin (Chapter 7), Motion Tween (Chapter 6), and filters (Chapter 5).

1. As tempting as it is to always rely on Adobe Flash to animate for us using the Motion Tween, there are times when keyframing is the only solution. One would think that animating the act of something melting might be the perfect job for a Shape Tween, but as we've seen earlier in this chapter, even Shape Hints aren't always reliable. So, let's see how to animate something melting using the tried and true technique of keyframe animation. In a new file, create four layers. The bottom three layers are primarily to enhance the overall look of the animation. The bottom layer provides a horizon line. The two layers above it create the reflection using the same method as used in the shiny 70's disco exercise. That leaves the top layer to do all the work.

2. Create a movie clip in the top layer. Within this clip, create two layers as shown in Figure 7-90.

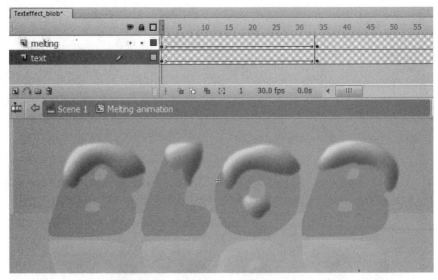

FIGURE 7-90   Inside the melting-text movie clip.

3. The bottom layer contains a simple piece of text that has been converted to its own movie clip and squeezed down with a simple Motion Tween.

4. The layer above it is where the melting takes place. Let's take a look at this layer.

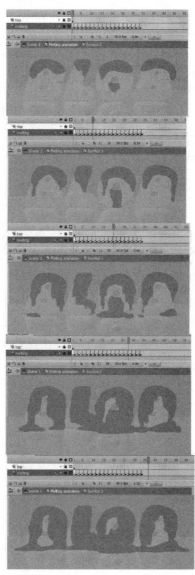

FIGURE 7-91 Keyframing the melting animation.

5. As you can see in Figure 7-91, as you move down the timeline, the melting progresses little by little until it pools together, forming a blob. The more frames you add in between, the smoother the animation. The sample in this exercise was animated on twos, but you can experiment animating on ones to see the difference. In fact, probably the best solution is to animate it on ones but to make each frame just slightly different from the one that preceded it. This requires a lot of patience, but the results are worth it. Fortunately, you have the **Onion Skin Outlines** tool to help you out.

6. With the hard part done, it's time to give this movie clip some added dimension. As you may have guessed by now, we do that using the **Bevel** and **Blur** filters.

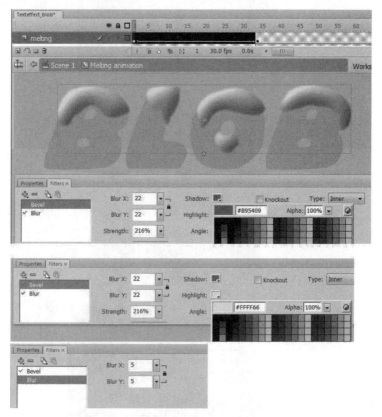

FIGURE 7-92   **Bevel, Blur** and **Shadow/Highlight** applied to the melting-text movie clip.

7. The next step is to squeeze the movie clip down just as you did with the text beneath it using a Motion Tween.

8. Finally, return to the main scene and apply one last **Bevel** filter to this main movie clip. See Figure 7-93.

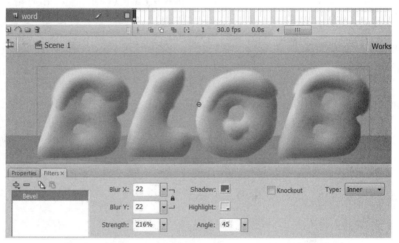

FIGURE 7-93 **Bevel** filter applied to the main movie clip.

SUMMARY

In this chapter, we covered the twelve principles of animation and their many uses. We learned that an animator is, for all intents and purposes, an actor who draws, and we learned that it is possible for a character's personality to be displayed onscreen when a scene's mood and a character's motivations are carefully considered. We continued to explore several animation tools available within the program to create different types of motion and special effects, and we learned that sometimes to get the most impressive results, it's best to use Motion Tweens in conjunction with traditional keyframe animation instead of relying on the software to do all the work. Last, we created several more advanced special effects using movie clips and filters.

EXERCISES

Exercise 7.1

Silent films are a great reference for animators. Rent a copy of Charlie Chaplin's film *City Lights* and note how the actor uses timing and exaggerated movements to let you know how he is feeling. Pay close attention to the many ways he uses his hands to express anything from "Wait a minute," "Hurry up," "Forget about it," "I'm through with you," and "Oh, boy!" You'll see Charlie frequently pointing, brushing himself off, wiping, tipping his hat, shrugging his shoulders, snapping his fingers in the air, adjusting his vest, and patting people on the back. The principle of anticipation is used to let the audience know what is about to happen. To let us know that the characters are about to fight, they pull their coats off halfway before being stopped. For a terrific example of cartoonlike behavior, watch the scene in the millionaire's house when the gunshot occurs. Charlie jumps on the couch, hides his face in the cushions like an ostrich in the sand, and then checks to see if his rear end is intact before climbing off the couch.

Exercise 7.2

Find some royalty-free music and a picture of a painting by Paul Klee, Piet Mondrian, or M.C. Escher. Recreate the painting using the **Brush** and **Line** tools, and convert the elements of the painting into symbols. Distribute the symbols to layers and animate them to the music. See how many of the animation principles you can apply with the basic shapes found in many of these paintings. If your animation is closely synchronized to the music, you will end up with a pretty slick music video.

Chapter 8 SHARING IS CARING

"When you reach for the stars you may not quite get one, but you won't come up with a handful of mud either."

—Leo Burnett

PREPARATION FOR DELIVERY

Congratulations! Your story has made the journey from a mere notion to a production complete with moving images, sound, and titles, ready for the world to see. Perhaps you already have an audience in mind, and simply want to know how to export your files in a format you can use. Or maybe you're looking to define your audience and need to know the steps required to getting your film seen. Either way, this chapter is for you.

Optimization

Before we get into exporting your files, it's important to ensure that your film will play as smoothly for your audience as it does for you on your home computer. This is especially important if the destination of your file is the World Wide Web. With so many variations of computers, memory choices, and cable speeds, it's impossible to know how your film will look to viewers watching your film on the Internet. That's why it's important to optimize your film as much as possible. Let's take a look at a few things you can do to optimize your film for export.

1. Reduce your file size by deleting unwanted layers, removing extra keyframes, and eliminating any stray items sitting outside of your stage. Choose **Show All** and view everything in **Outline** mode. This will help you see any hidden items.

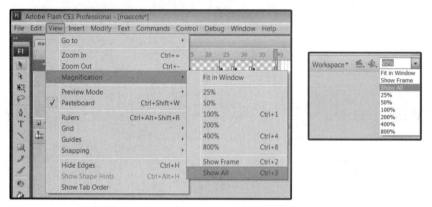

FIGURE 8-1   View ▶ Magnification ▶ Show All.

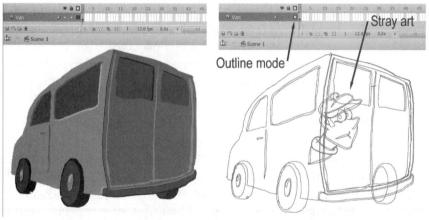

FIGURE 8-2   Hidden item revealed in **Outline** Mode.

2. Look for any artwork that could use some cleaning up. Perhaps a certain asset has more points than it needs, or its curves aren't as smooth as they

could be. Double-click its symbol until you can select the art in its raw state. Go to **Modify ▶ Shape ▶ Optimize**. Adjust the slider as necessary. You can undo the last setting and experiment with different settings until you find a solution you're happy with.

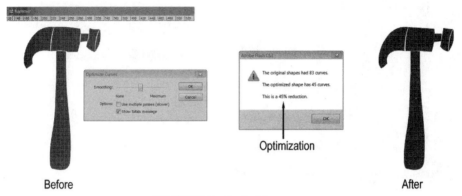

Before   After

FIGURE 8-3   Optimizing curves.

3. It's easy to lose track of assets you no longer need when you're in the process of revising your artwork or adjusting an animation. When you've reached the point of completion, it's a good idea to delete all unused symbols from your Library to lessen the file size. You can save it as a different version or filename if you're hesitant to throw away any artwork that could be useful in the future. This is how to do it:

a. Open your Library (**Ctrl+L**).
b. Shift-select all the items in your Library.
c. From the triangle in the upper-right corner of your Library, choose **Select Unused Items**.
d. Adobe® Flash® will highlight all items not currently being used in your film. Click on the tiny **trash can** icon at the bottom of your library.
e. Answer **Yes** or **No** when the pop-ups appear.
f. Save your file under a new name.

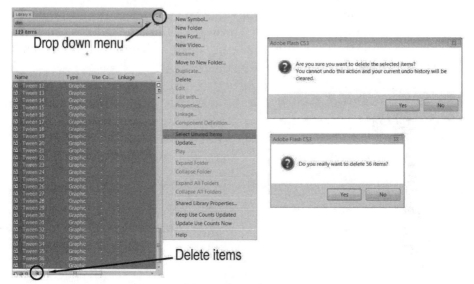

FIGURE 8-4   Deleting unused items from your Library.

4. Movies exported from Adobe Flash will only play audio sitting on the main scene's timeline. This means that any audio you buried deep inside a character's head when animating dialogue will not be heard. It will, however, add to the file's overall size. After you've copied and pasted a character's dialogue onto the main scene's timeline, remember to delete it from within the character's symbol. To further reduce your file's size, you can choose to customize the compression for each sound file individually from within the Library, or you can assign the same compression to all of the audio simultaneously, using the technique covered in step 5.

5. First, let's see how you would compress sound files one at a time from within your library.

   a. Open your Library and select a sound file. Click the **Sound Properties** icon at the bottom of your Library.

FIGURE 8-5   Opening the **Sound Properties**.

b. The **Sound Properties** panel shows your original compression setting, its size, and options to test or replace your old sound with a new one.

c. Click the **Compression** drop-down menu, and make the selections indicated in Figure 8-6. The sound file's new information will appear beneath your choices. Click **OK** to accept.

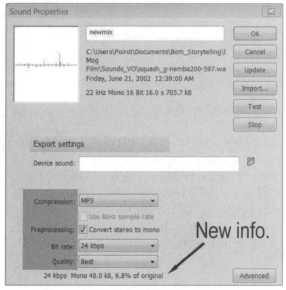

FIGURE 8-6   The **Sound Properties** pop-up panel.

6. The **Publish Settings** panel is quite powerful. As mentioned in step 4, you can have Adobe Flash compress all of your audio at once prior to export. You can also compress the entire movie, generate a size report for a detailed view of your assets, and test the movie for a preview. From the top menu, go to **File ▶ Publish Settings** and click the **Flash** tab. Click the **Set** button for **Audio stream**, and choose the settings shown in Figure 8-7. Click **OK** to close the panels. Test the movie and listen to the audio quality.

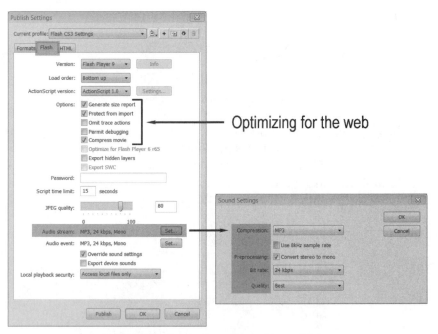

FIGURE 8-7   Audio compression settings.

7. Each time you test a movie via **Control ▶ Test Movie**, you have the option to see how large your file is and how long it is. This can be quite useful to monitor your progress and to make any changes to your art as you work on your film. It will also be how you check your space savings after following the steps above. To call up the **Bandwidth Profiler**, open a file that you've been working on, and test the movie. From the pop-up panel's top menu, go to **View ▶ Bandwidth Profiler**.

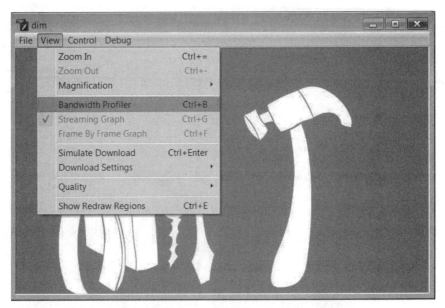

FIGURE 8-8   Accessing the **Bandwidth Profiler**.

Here you will see some familiar statistics pertaining to your film as well as your timeline presented as a graph. As shown in Figure 8-9, bars rising above the red line indicate the chance that you have certain elements that may be weighing your file down at that point. This may be inconsequential since you will most likely be converting your film to a self-contained Quicktime® file, but it's good information to have if you plan to upload your film to your Web site as a .swf.

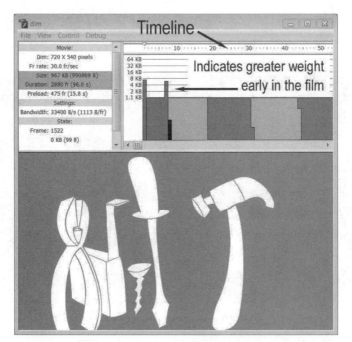

FIGURE 8-9   The **Bandwidth Profiler**.

8. A size report lists every single frame in your film and its size in bytes. To generate a size report, go to **File ▶ Publish Settings**, click the box next to **Generate size report**, and click **Publish** at the bottom.

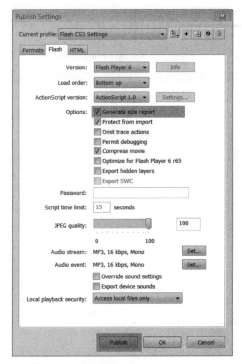

FIGURE 8-10 Generating size report.

The nice thing about this report is that you can pinpoint exactly which frames could benefit from some size reduction, thus eliminating any guesswork on your part.

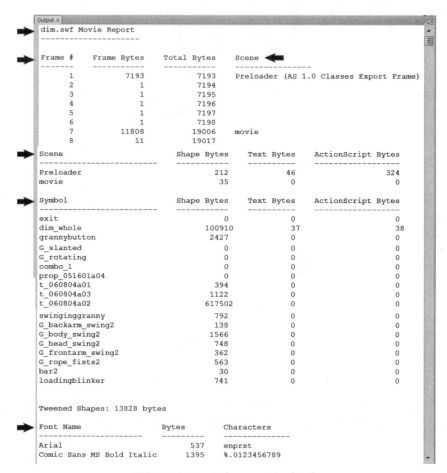

FIGURE 8-11 A size report in detail.

EXPORTING FROM ADOBE FLASH

Now that you have optimized your film, you're ready for the next phase. The first step is to get your film out of Adobe Flash and into a format you can use for editing. If your entire film was small enough to fit into one Adobe Flash file, then you've already taken care of the editing process, and these next few steps may be all you need to get your film out there. If not, you'll need to export each clip as its own video and edit it afterward. Here's how to convert your film from an Adobe Flash file to a self-contained movie.

From a Mac:

1. Go to **File ▶ Export ▶ ExportMovie**.
2. Name your film and save as **Type: Quicktime** (*.mov). Click **Save**.
3. Choose the settings as indicated in Figures 8-12 and 8-13.

View export settings   Specify settings

FIGURE 8-12   Quicktime® settings when exporting from a Mac.

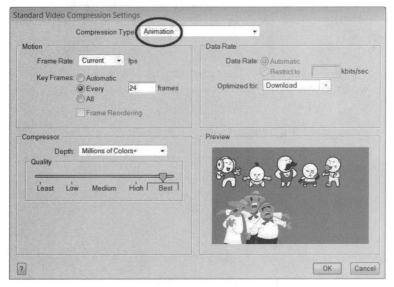

FIGURE 8-13   Compression pop-up panel.

4. Click **Export**. Your film is now ready for either importing into a video editor or burning to a DVD.

From a PC:

1. Go to **File ▶ Export ▶ ExportMovie**.
2. Name your film and save as **Type: Quicktime** (*.mov). Click **Save**.
3. Choose the settings as indicated in Figures 8-14 and 8-15.

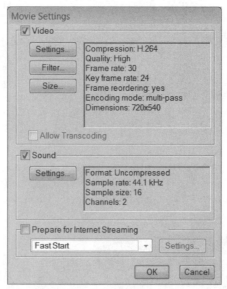

FIGURE 8-14   Quicktime® settings when exporting from a PC.

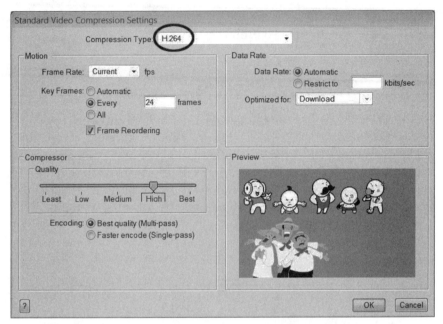

FIGURE 8-15   **Compression** pop-up panel with H.264 compression setting.

4. Click **Export**. Your film is now ready for either importing into a video editor or burning to a DVD.

EDITING YOUR CLIPS

If you're on a Mac, you can import your Quicktime movies into iMovie®, arrange your clips correspondingly, and choose a file format that best suits your destination, be it a DVD, iPod®, or Web. Experiment with different settings until you find the one with the combination of sound quality, image resolution, and frame rate that suits your needs.

If you're on a PC, you can import your Quicktime movies into Moviemaker®, arrange your clips accordingly, and follow the same procedure as mentioned above. Both iMovie and Moviemaker offer the option to import your sound separately. This could come in handy if, for example, your film was separated into several scenes or Adobe Flash files, preventing you from incorporating a single music track. Now you can add your music soundtrack separately and have it play all the way through your film.

PROMOTION AND MARKETING

Philosopher Bishop George Berkeley once asked, "If a tree falls in a forest and no one is around to hear it, does it make a sound?" Although this philosophical riddle was meant to investigate the relationship between perception and reality, it could also apply to your film. Ask yourself: If you spent all your time making your film, and there's no one around to see it, will it fulfill its purpose? Most likely, the answer is no. The harsh reality is that if no one knows about your film, then it won't be seen.

NETWORKING

Building a buzz around your film is a key element to getting your film seen. A good place to start is your home computer. Begin by building a Web site dedicated to your film. Place a short movie trailer on the homepage. By using bits of footage from your film, you can quickly put together a short teaser to whet a visitor's appetite. Watch some examples of book trailers on the Web to see how still images are combined with text to generate interest. The increasing popularity of motion comics shows just how creative you can be with limited animation, still imagery, and a few well-made special effects. If building a Web site is not feasible, register for a free blog and post a compelling 1–2 paragraph synopsis describing your film's content, its importance, and anything else that will grab the viewer's attention. Sprinkle in some early concept art and production stills to give your future audience a visual taste. Upload a "making of" video showing how a particular scene or background was made. Make a small blooper reel just for fun and post it as well. The more your audience is included in the process, the more emotionally invested they will be. Once you've made a place for people to go, join several of the many social networking sites that are on the Web, and let people know about your film's destination page. Sites like www.deviantart.com let you upload film clips and artwork for the entire world to see in a friendly and supportive artist's environment. The immediate feedback that you receive will help you forge relationships with other artists and keep you inspired. Professional networking sites like www.linkedin.com have groups you can join and discussion boards where you can talk about your film and participate in other people's conversations. You can create a fan page on www.facebook.com and provide updates on your film's progress or screenings. For more frequent updates, try www.twitter.com. The Web is chock-full of sites for filmmakers and artists. Find ones you like and be an active participant in their forums. Make genuine comments on people's blogs. The more active you are on the Web, the more visible your film will be.

Speaking of being visible, it's important that people can put a face to the film. As its main representative, you play a crucial role in showing that there is a real human being behind this film. That's where attending industry conferences, film and storytelling festivals, and comic book conventions comes in. The people you meet at these events are your peers, potential clients, and audience. They love storytelling as much as you do and would love to hear about your project and share theirs as well.

DISTRIBUTION

Your distribution methods depend largely on what you hope to accomplish with your film. If it is part of a larger sales presentation or performance, then you probably plan on traveling with it as you tour. You can then offer it for sale on DVD. You could additionally sell it on your Web site using Paypal®. If your film is one in a series, then you could pitch it to a network or to buyers at conventions like MIPCOM or MIPJUNIOR, two events designed specifically for showcasing and purchasing television properties. If your immediate goal is to gain exposure, then you can easily upload your film to some of the many video-sharing sites available like www.youtube.com, www.vimeo.com, or www.dailymotion.com. But be aware that some traditional film festivals will not accept your film if it has previously screened on the Web. Video-sharing sites also come with their own sets of pros and cons. Some pros include wide visibility, ease of upload, and immediate feedback. Cons are poor video quality, pop-up ads interfering with the viewing experience, or potential for copyright infringement—it is possible for others to download your film, claim it as their own, or even sell it as a compilation.

As an alternative, you can approach your local cable television channels, libraries, and universities to see if your film could play as part of a larger screening of films. Everyone loves a rising star, and your biggest supporters may be right in your own backyard.

FILM FESTIVALS

There's no greater feeling for an independent filmmaker than to see your short film play on the big screen. Film festivals are a terrific way for a filmmaker to gain exposure, and a site like www.withoutabox.com is a great place to start. Open a free account and start browsing the thousands of film festivals playing throughout the year. Highlight those that match your film's genre, and take note of their entry fees and submission requirements. Assemble a monetary budget beforehand and be selective by choosing the festivals that offer the most bang for your buck. A festival's value can be determined by its location, the number of categories for which your film is eligible, or whether your film's acceptance qualifies it for an Academy Award® nomination. Remember that acceptance is not guaranteed, so it's in your best interest to pick the festivals for which you believe your film is most qualified. That requires you to be as objective as possible when playing back your film. Maybe your two-minute Peruvian folktale isn't what a large film festival like Sundance is looking for right now. No problem. There are plenty of other festivals around the world to choose from.

So what do you do when your film is accepted? Write a press release, and send it to your local newspaper and any Web site or blog devoted to the subject of your film. Include your film's synopsis, the dates of your screenings, your contact information, and any information that you believe make your film relevant to their column, Web site, or blog. Make them as excited about your film as you are. One of the best perks of having your film accepted is the opportunity to travel to the cities playing your film. Though this can become quite expensive, you owe it to yourself to at least make one trip. When you do, ask local businesses if they're willing to post flyers in their windows. Place visually stunning postcards in the theater where attendees can grab one. Hand out business cards as you make contacts. Keep a journal, take photographs, make new friends, enjoy your stay—these experiences are the fruits of your labor. Be prepared to talk about your film by having a two-sentence log line that magnetically describes your film to those who ask. For sample log lines, visit www.netflix.com or www.moviefone.com and browse their selections. Read the brief descriptions of films you enjoy or have a similar theme to yours. Take note of how excitement for each movie is built with just a few words.

ONLINE CONTESTS

Online contests are another vehicle for exposure and recognition, but should be approached with caution. Before entering your work, read the contest's terms of agreement carefully, and make certain that you retain full rights to your creation. Occasionally, the company sponsoring the contest will want to reserve the right to use your film for promotional purposes. Ultimately, it's up to you whether you want to allow that. Some contests may pose an entry fee. Use your budget to determine whether it's worth the investment. As with all things on the Web, the more you know about the source, the better off you'll be.

SUMMARY

This chapter was devoted to getting the most out of your animated film. We explored various techniques for optimization, the many settings for export, and the numerous ways to promote, distribute, and sell your work. When all is said and done, you should be very proud of your accomplishment, because for every individual who completes this adventure, there are many more who do not. If this is your first time making an animated film, start small—a couple of minutes at the very most. To create your production schedule, use a festival's submission deadline or upcoming convention. Most importantly, have fun and remember why you wanted to tell your story in the first place.

EXERCISES

Exercise 8.1

Visit Web sites of current feature films playing in your area and study how they package their promotion. Do they have downloadable desktop wallpapers? Do they have a subscription to their mailing list with offers to receive an updated newsletter? Do they have a cast and plot breakdown? Is there a link to a store where fans can order T-shirts, mugs, or other film paraphernalia? Some studios will send out media kits containing production stills and press releases. Request a copy and review it for content and overall design.

Exercise 8.2

Pick an overarching theme from your film and design a promotional campaign around it. Include a Web site interface, letterhead, envelopes, logo, business cards, poster, and flyer. Be sure they all tie together visually, and are consistent with the look of your film. As a bonus, think of how a podcast can serve to promote your art or film. Could you have monthly interviews with guests? Are there topics about your craft worth discussing? Could you release your film in short installments to build a fan base?

9 Chapter ONE-ON-ONE WITH THE PROS

Q & A WITH LINDA SIMENSKY, VICE PRESIDENT OF CHILDREN'S PROGRAMMING, PBS

What do you do?

I am the Vice President of Children's Programming for PBS. I oversee the development and production of children's series that are distributed by PBS to local stations. We work on everything from the big vision of what our goals are with the programming all the way down to working out the details of when the series will be fed out to stations in the national feed. In the course of doing that, my department and I work with producers to develop and produce series, look at pitches, look at series in progress, and talk with the programmers at stations about which shows are working for them.

What's a typical day like for you?

I spend a fair amount of time with my department and my colleagues from other departments at PBS, particularly with the Interactive department, since all of our projects have a presence on the Web as well. In the course of a typical day, I work on series, read scripts and pitches, look at material for development, talk with producers of our series, talk to people calling with questions about developing series, talk to programmers at stations, troubleshoot and deal with issues as they come up, and in the midst of that, try to keep up with what is going on in the animation and kids' industries.

Describe the path that led you to where you are now.

I was always interested in animation and children's programming, mainly as a viewer. I loved watching cartoons when I was young, and I never stopped watching them. I was always interested in the programming side, realizing at a young age that I was a better viewer than I was animator. During college, I had a summer job in the early 80s at Nickelodeon and went back there to work in the programming department. I helped start up the animation department there and became the first head of animation development at Nick. I worked on *Rugrats*, *Doug*, *Ren and Stimpy*, *Rocko's Modern Life*, and a number of pilots up through *Hey Arnold*. In 1995, I moved over to Cartoon Network to head up programming and eventually I started up their in-house animation development department. I worked on the early series there—*Dexter's Laboratory*, *Johnny Bravo*, *Ed, Edd n Eddy*, *Courage the Cowardly Dog*, *Samurai Jack*, all the way up through *Foster's Home for Imaginary Friends*. After my son turned two and started watching television, I became much more interested in preschool programming and what he was watching. That is what led me to PBS.

Who or what inspires you?

I am inspired by independent animated shorts and illustration, for the most part, although any animation from any era and from any country is interesting to me. I also like children's books, as well as any sort of technological innovation.

Where do you see the future of your industry headed?

People have been debating the future of television lately, but we are mostly just shifting from one screen over to many opportunities to watch content on many different screens. I think kids' content, particularly educational content, will become more interactive as more of it emerges on newer and more interactive platforms. Story and character will remain as important as ever—I think there is always going to be a need for engaging character-driven narrative content on any platform.

What suggestions do you have for someone wanting to enter your field?

People interested in working in kids' programming need to be passionate about it. They need to keep watching it steadily to be familiar with everything going on in the industry, and they need to allow themselves to form opinions, understand storytelling, and have a vision for what they'd like to do. They should start out at the entry level with enthusiasm and motivation. It is important for them to see their first jobs in the industry as learning experiences and chances to meet people and learn as much as possible.

What do you like most about your job?

I like seeing kids fall in love with the characters on our air. I also like being able to shape the direction PBS Kids' programming is going. I started at PBS with the idea that the series on PBS Kids needed to be both as entertaining as possible and as educational as possible, and I have been working steadily toward that goal for several years now. It has been extremely fulfilling to see us push the series in that direction and to see the success that PBS Kids has been having.

I also enjoy working with the extremely intelligent, highly motivated people at PBS whom I learn from every day.

What do you like least about your job?

We spend a great deal of time dealing with funding issues and encountering the consequences of limited funds. That can be frustrating at times, although these days, I sense that every company is dealing with these issues.

What are you working on now?

The next series that we have coming out is a preschool science series based on the Cat in the Hat science library, called *The Cat in the Hat Knows a Lot About That*. We also have a series for kids aged 6–9 coming out called *WildKratts*, featuring animated versions of Chris and Martin Kratt of *Kratts' Creatures* fame. I am working on four pilots and development for future years. I spend a great deal of time talking with the Interactive department so these series will all have interesting approaches on the Web and emerging platforms such as mobile phones.

If you don't currently work in Adobe Flash, how can you imagine its technology serving you in the future?

Most of our 2D series are in Adobe Flash or in programs similar to Adobe Flash. I think it's been amazing how quickly Adobe Flash has become a standard broadcast production technique. We require that all of our PBS Kids series be innovative in some way and some are innovative in their production technologies, such as Henson's Motion Capture Digital Puppetry®, which The Jim Henson Company uses to produce *Sid the Science Kid*. I'd like to think that limited production budgets or even limited time to produce series will be the catalysts that lead to innovation in production.

Q & A WITH JAMES REITANO, CREATIVE DIRECTOR, TFU STUDIOS

What do you do?
I'm a commercial animator/illustrator.

What's a typical day like for you?
Check e-mails, follow up on invoices, and basically regiment the day according to my obligations.

Describe the path that led you to where you are now.
I've always drawn, and was mystified by animation/effects since I was young kid, but my biggest draw was to storytelling. This led me directly to comics and books. I was reading sci-fi and horror novels when I was really young, and this led me to attempting my own. I wrote about 30 pages of a screenplay when I was a kid, and eventually attempted to make it in comic form. Comics and animation were an accessible way for me to do these things that were otherwise outside my grasp. Just grab a pad of paper and start.

Who or what inspires you?
I get inspired just hearing someone tell a great story. Or seeing some awesome piece of design or architecture. I'll immediately think of the individual behind that creation, and what the process was.

Where do you see the future of your industry headed?
I think the means as to which this stuff gets done, whether it's technology /and or labor is going to change drastically. We're undergoing a major shift in terms of labor in the first world, and the animation/entertainment industry won't be an exception. One thing that will not change is personal experience and how your storytelling draws from that. In other words, a person from Tibet's experience/ story will always be there. The methods of telling that story are always going to be secondary.

What suggestions do you have for someone wanting to enter your field?
As is the case with anything, be prepared to work hard and stay focused. Those are the two most important traits to have, especially in the animation business. Most folks I know who have sustained long careers have that ability to focus

on a single project for a long period of time. You'll be having numerous days when you'll be sick and tired of your project, and you really need that ability to persevere to completion.

What do you like most about your job?

The challenge and the surprise of the daily work upload. It never seems to get monotonous. And it's always great to hear clients get excited about their project coming back exceeding expectations. Animation requires you to dream up a world taken from words on a page, and there's a great feeling in making something from nothing.

What do you like least about your job?

The hours tend to be long, and can be trying on personal relationships. In working with a group or organization, more times than not, the process and the politics start to overshadow the actual goal.

What are you working on now?

Right now I'm working on some titles for Spike TV, as well as developing comic/packaging for a hip hop star. Some other commercial animation work as well, but also a comic series based on my teenage years as a graffiti artist.

How can you imagine Adobe Flash technology serving you in the future?

It's always going to be handy for organic animated elements as well as a quick way to test and preview animations and timings. I love the fact that I can just sketch basic stick figures and time out a potential sequence.

What's a tip or trick in Adobe Flash that you'd like to share with others?

Never underestimate the power of bitmap fills and textures. You can get some pretty cool results.

What feature in Adobe Flash would you most like to see added?

I do miss the programming simplicity of it all. It's become a powerful development program, but, I wish it was still easy to create a quick mini-application just using a few buttons.

Q & A WITH BOB HARPER

What do you do?
I am a cartoonist/animator.

What's a typical day like for you?
I wake up early, look in the mirror, and decide if this is the day I launch my secret horde of robots to take over the world, then I am awakened by my kids who need me to take them to school. It's then animating full-time at a television network. I then return home, play with the kids, and get back to my plans of world domination (or at least work on my own animation projects).

Describe the path that led you to where you are now.
I would say it was a corkscrew path with rollercoaster ups and downs. Definitely not the traditional way. I am mostly self-taught, bugging other professionals for help and advice.

Who or what inspires you?
Rocky and Bullwinkle, Mad magazine, Monty Python, and the Sex Pistols.

Where do you see the future of your industry headed?
A sharp divide between independent/creator-driven work and branded corporate product.

What suggestions do you have for someone wanting to enter your field?
Don't! Get a real job! Seriously though, discover what it is you truly want out of this business and what it takes to achieve it and GO FOR IT—but have fun!

What do you like most about your job?
The free snacks! And I guess discovering new ways to solve problems.

What do you like least about your job?
The shackles and many hours away from home.

What are you working on now?
Personally, an animated feature; my day job is on an animated television show.

If you work with Adobe Flash, what's a tip or trick in Adobe Flash that you'd like to share with others?

None! My secrets are mine! Well, I guess it would be safe to tell folks to be sure and explore every single window and tool Adobe Flash has, you'll never know what you will discover as a great asset in your work.

What feature in Adobe Flash would you most like to see added?

The **Animate Better** button has been overlooked for over a decade. Besides that I would like to see better integration of other Adobe® programs into or with Adobe Flash player such as the Adobe® Illustrator® blend function.

Q & A WITH SAM CHI

What do you do?

I am an animator and artist who uses Adobe Flash to create animation for TV shows and commercials, and I currently live in Los Angeles. I've worked on several seasons of *Foster's Home for Imaginary Friends* and have provided animation for Esurance, Happy Tree Friends, and *Harvey Birdman.*

What's a typical day like for you?

Most days, I will be on the computer working on various projects with programs such as Adobe Flash, Adobe Photoshop, and Adobe Illustrator. Usually, I'll receive a batch of scenes to do, which I will animate according to the storyboard and animatic.

Describe the path that led you to where you are now.

I've always loved to create things and bring them to life, so it made sense for me to end up in the field of animation. I was introduced to Adobe Flash during my senior year in high school and was taught traditional animation at the Savannah College of Art and Design. Afterward, I was able to combine the skills I've learned with my knowledge of the Adobe Flash program to become an animator.

Who or what inspires you?

I am greatly inspired by many of the talented artists working in this industry. This includes the animators that I have worked with over the years, some of whom have taught me a lot about animation, as well as artists that are involved in concept art, illustration, and graphic novels. To be able to create interesting characters and to tell compelling stories in any artistic field is something I admire.

Where do you see the future of your industry headed?

I think there is potential for a lot of growth. The nice thing about Adobe Flash is that it can be used in many different ways. You can use it to make feature films, television shows, commercials, video games, Web animations, interactive illustrations, etc. There are many paths to choose from.

What suggestions do you have for someone wanting to enter your field?

Being an animator involves a lot of self motivation and hard work. You'll need to practice constantly and be open to learning new things. It also helps to go to a good art school, where you can benefit from the experience of other artists.

What do you like most about your job?

I enjoy being creative when it comes to animating something. I also like the variety of artistic styles, which keeps things interesting.

What do you like least about your job?

The crazy deadlines.

What are you working on now?

I currently do freelance work for a bunch of different studios as well as occasional independent projects.

If you work with Adobe Flash, what's a tip or trick in Adobe Flash that you'd like to share with others?

Save and save often. Also, as with all programs, be aware of Adobe Flash strengths and limitations.

What feature in Adobe Flash would you most like to see added?

I would generally like to see better drawing tools in Adobe Flash. Perhaps an easier way to organize the different symbols and assets. As animation projects progressively get larger and more complex, future versions of Adobe Flash need to be powerful enough to handle the increased workload.

Q & A WITH BARNEY SALTZBERG

What do you do?
I write and illustrate picture books as well as write and record songs for children.

What's a typical day like for you?
The gym, walk the dogs, and in my studio. Depending on what stage I'm at, I'm either writing and illustrating something new which I'm hoping to sell, or doing finished art or editing from something which I would typically be working with an editor or art director on.

Describe the path that led you to where you are now.
I read a picture book by William Steig and fell in love with the idea that beautiful art and a wonderful story could be contained in such a small, beautiful package in the shape of a book. I dreamed of one day making my own books like that and living on a farm where I would create my books in an old converted barn. Well, half of that dream came true. I'm still waiting for the barn.

Who or what inspires you?
Early on, Jim Henson, both from his character development to his use of humor to get points across and his genuine silliness! At this point, being on the planet inspires me. I get ideas constantly from things I see and hear, and of course things I'm feeling.

Where do you see the future of your industry headed?
DIGITAL WORLD.

I know people my age shudder, but I'm inspired by digital technology. People my age are worried that books will be dead. I think there is a real possibility over the next few years that even picture books will be digital. Given that I write stories, draw my own art, and write music and songs, I think digital books would be a perfect way to combine all of what I do in a really compelling, interesting, and entertaining way.

What suggestions do you have for someone wanting to enter your field?
Focus on STORY. That in and of itself is what this is all about. Even something as basic as *Avatar* illustrates my point. Yes, it's pioneering new technology, but

if the story didn't hold up, we wouldn't care. There are plenty of movies and books with an amazing look, but people forget that the story is what it's all about at the end of the day. So, in my field, read, read, and read. Write, write, and write! Also, leave your ego at home in the closet and be open to hearing what editors have to say.

What do you like most about your job?
The freedom to get up and go into my studio and create on a daily basis. Plus for me, visiting schools and meeting the people who read my books and sing my songs.

What do you like least about your job?
Uncertainty of the financial side. No regular paychecks. No guarantee of work. (Which seems to be prevalent these days in most fields!)

What are you working on now?
I'm finishing sketches for a book about my giant puppy, Arlo, who can't catch a ball to save his life!

If you don't currently work with Adobe Flash, how can you imagine its technology serving you in the future?
I would love to see my characters from my books animated to help make book trailers.

Q & A WITH JEFF ZIKRY

What do you do?
I'm a character animator. I work in 2D (hand drawn and Adobe Flash) and 3D.

What's a typical day like for you?
It depends. Some jobs require different mind-sets. Sometimes quality dictates schedule, and other times speed is the more important variable. First things first . . . coffee . . . lots of coffee. Next, I try to lay out my day. I find that I am the most productive in the morning, so I try to get in early. I do most of my heavy lifting first. Anything that requires problem solving, scene planning, or animation that is open to my own interpretation, I attack first. I generally key

out my scenes before lunch. That way most of the acting is solved early on. The rest of the day tends to be second nature.

Describe the path that led you to where you are now.

When I graduated college, internships and jobs had just about all dried up. Disney was going through its first round of layoffs, and there was no room for a college student. Fortunately, TV animation was on the rise at the studios. Until that time, most TV animated shows were being done overseas. Adobe Flash had been designed for the Web, but a few people who saw its potential had paved the way and had given me a career that I hadn't thought about. I had my first production job at Comedy Central's *Kid Notorious*, a show that lasted one season, but it started my education on the ins and outs of TV production. I had difficulty that year since I had been trained in full-feature style. I never really understood the economy of animation until I came to my next job. *Kid Notorious* gave me a slightly better resume to open the doors at Cartoon Network. I was hired on to *Foster's Home for Imaginary Friends*. At the time, I could point out in detail the scenes that Glen Keane or Andeas Deja had animated, but I had never heard of Craig McCracken, Eric Pringle, or Craig Kellman, who were not just important to my education as an artist but were well respected in the animation community. It took me a while, but I learned that less is more, and the overall idea was more important than just the scene I was working on.

At the time, I was still donating my time, working on projects that I felt would help me grow. I never understood artists complaining about low pay or doing free work. In my opinion, you can always get something in return. I spent a year on two different projects where I wasn't paid. And both had significant influence on my abilities. In fact, I recently took a significant pay cut to work on a project that excited me.

Who or what inspires you?

I have always been influenced and inspired by acting that doesn't feel like it was pulled out of a book. When I spend time studying acting, I usually look at live-action film making and actors that create different mannerisms in body language or facial tics. In my opinion, acting should feel natural, not normal. If that makes any sense. For example, Jack Nicholson is a unique character, but pretty much the same in every role he plays. Actors like Heath Ledger and Johnny Depp seem to put the character's needs and wants over their own. I love it when you watch a movie and only halfway through it do you finally recognize an actor. To me, that actor really pulled it off!

Where do you see the future of your industry headed?

Not too sure. I see much change; however, it just seems like there are ten different lead characters per film now, all with character arcs. I grew up watching movies like *Raiders of the Lost Ark* and *Star Wars*. I feel like we are in serious need of another Indiana Jones. In other words, a story told from one person's point of view. I would like to see a little more concentration on the one lead character and his or her connection to the audience.

What suggestions do you have for someone wanting to enter your field?

BE SURE! It takes a lot of work and dedication, not just to get into animation for a few years, but to survive long-term. It isn't a 9 to 5 job, and if you plan to have a family, it helps to have them on board. Also, learn to distance yourself from your work. You not only have to do your best, but be prepared to redo your work to suit the needs of the film. Remember, what you feel is right is only opinion.

What do you like most about your job?

Sounds cliché, but I love bringing a character to life. Some people are all about the drawing, and I do love the drawing, there are different breeds of animator, and I always fell under an "acting first" mentality. That's first and foremost, but I also love the people and the work environment as well. I can't see myself wearing slacks and going to an office talking about reality TV around the water cooler. People in animation generally aren't watchers. . . they're doers! I feel at home here.

What do you like least about your job?

The simple fact is that it is and always will be a business. About 90% of the time, money dictates quality. But still, I wouldn't be happy doing anything else.

What are you working on now?

Just finished working on a *Tom and Jerry* DVD, and now I'm on a first-run series for Comedy Central.

If you work with Adobe Flash, what's a tip or trick in Adobe Flash that you'd like to share with others?

I would probably have to show you. Mostly technical tricks I've learned along the way, and they are a bit tough to explain.

What feature in Adobe Flash would you most like to see added?
The ability to handle larger file sizes with ease would be nice. Generally, more than three characters and a background tends to bog down your computer no matter how much RAM you have. I think it's something in the code. Also, more accurate drawing tools.

Q & A WITH DAVE REDL, FAMILYPANTS.COM

What do you do?
From 9 to 5, I'm Animation Director at Funny Garbage, a design studio in New York City. From 5 to 9, I animate *Family Pants* [familypants.com], a cartoon series of my own creation as well as draw a political comic strip called *Angie* [angiecomics.blogspot.com]. In addition I supplement income as a gun-for-hire freelancer in animation and cartooning [daveredl.com].

What's a typical day like for you?
An early, long commute allows for time on the bus and a touch of delirium from lack of sleep to jot down creative notes and ideas for future projects. The professional and personal sides complement each other as techniques used on weekend work finds their way into weekday work and vise versa. "Dave, how would you animate this project?" "Well, it turns out I just did something like that a month ago..." Or a canceled client request becomes my next weekend *Family Pants* technique rather than being tossed away. Sometimes *Family Pants* serves as a "I told you it can be done" experiment from my day job. Some nights are late and weekends are early to finish all the extra work.

Describe the path that led you to where you are now.
Professionally, I worked as cartoonist for King Features Syndicate drawing *Popeye* and *Betty Boop*, among other timeless characters, right out of college. I got my feet wet with the big business of licensing, cartooning for print, and adapting to various styles. Eventually I co-wrote, co-directed, and animated two *Popeye* pilots called *Popeye Untold*, which rekindled the animation bug in me. My belief the Internet was a new frontier for comic strips and animation was not shared by my superiors, so I left for Funny Garbage, who believed as I did. At Funny Garbage, I animated many cartoon shorts for CartoonNetwork.com's *Web Premiere Toons*. I eventually worked my way up to animation director and continued creating animation for new media.

Personally, I created a comic strip called *Family Pants* with intention to syndicate it online to Web sites, which I believed to become the eventual "digital newspaper." I took one comic strip and used it as a storyboard to create a 30-second animation for the *Family Pants* Web site. It immediately became the most popular part of the site. Some people didn't even know I HAD comic strips! But I kept the comics part alive along with building a couple of games when I learned basic Adobe Flash Action Script. After making a *Family Pants* 22-minute TV pilot for DVD, I returned to comic strips and even created a new comic strip, *Angie*, for it requires less of a 100% focus. In other words, you can eat dinner, watch TV, or drive a car while thinking of new comic strip gags. You can't animate while driving, which may or may not be illegal in some states!

Who or what inspires you?

Classic Slapstick and animation:

Tex Avery, the Three Stooges, Laurel and Hardy, the Marx Brothers, Charlie Chaplin.

Modern TV Animation Humor:

South Park, *Family Guy*

Classic TV Humor:

I Love Lucy, *Dick Van Dyke*, *The Honeymooners*

Economized Animation:

UPA cartoons, UPA inspired Disney cartoons (like their *Space and Beyond* series), John Sutherland Cartoons, *Roger Ramjet*, *Rocky and Bullwinkle*, *The Flintstones* (Season 1), early *Pink Panther*

If stranded on a deserted island, the quick list or my favorite three things that deserve to be singled out:

Bugs Bunny, *Seinfeld*, *Underdog*

(I can talk all day about these three...)

Where do you see the future of your industry headed?

The Internet. The future of all media will be the Internet. If you don't have one already, in the future you'll have one device that sits in the corner of your home which has internet access. From there you'll watch over air TV, cable TV or home video, listen to the radio, stream music, or listen to your personal music collection, read newspapers, magazines, blogs, Web sites, other periodicals and books, play games online or off, and communicate with voice-only or video conversations.

For all of this new media, a cartoonist and animator's services may be required. Perhaps to illustrate a cartoon for design, entertainment, instruction, education, sales, social networking, or editorial purposes. Perhaps to animate that cartoon simply because in new media cartoons can move, while in old media they cannot. In addition, production assistance for those busy cartoonists and animators will be required, especially for animation, since that craft is so time consuming.

What suggestions do you have for someone wanting to enter your field?

For animation, learn print cartooning. For cartooning, learn Adobe Flash and traditional animation. And for both learn new media, writing, and business. The more you can spread your weight out, the more likely you won't fall through thin ice. Artists specialize in areas because they can, not because they want to. For example, I've noticed every graduate wants to be a character designer. I won't tell you to give up, because like the lottery, you never know, but understand that 99% of the time, you'll never be hired for what you really want. You get the job because you can do a tiny thing that no one else can. After you hang there for a while, you build trust and someone eventually asks, "Hey, who can we get to design these characters?" And then, there you go.

What do you like most about your job?

Art.

Drawing, cartooning, writing, animating, designing, audio editing, voices acting, production meetings about animation process... every aspect of production. Even the really boring production work! It provides an opportunity to listen to music and drown out the world.

What do you like least about your job?

People.

Some clients or producers have no understanding of animation or cartooning and don't care to learn, which forces you to spend more time teaching them than doing work. While teaching can be fun, it's only that way with those who want to learn. As with any job, higher ups who don't appreciate what you do create a kind of class warfare: the aristocrats against the commoners, which turns into office politics manipulating others to see the light. And that's not fun for anybody.

What are you working on now?
Speaking of politics, *Angie,* a political comic strip found at www.angiecomics. blogspot.com.

If you work with Adobe Flash, what's a tip or trick in Adobe Flash that you'd like to share with others?
There's a few but with Adobe Flash and equipment constantly updating, many tricks that work today won't work tomorrow. So with that in mind, the best tip would be to stay on top of Adobe Flash integration with other programs such as After Effects®.

In a big production, I keep all my Adobe Flash files organized by backgrounds. So all the scenes in a kitchen would be kept together in a single file, organized by using Adobe Flash's Scene window. The way Adobe Flash works with its symbols and library, if I update the toaster in the kitchen, all scenes that have that toaster become updated.

I'd render out each scene from Adobe Flash separately as a SWF. (You'll need to stay away from movie clip symbols and action script. There's a trick for that too, but that's a detailed one!) Then I organize all the SWFs into the correct sequence in After Effects® and render out a Quicktime® from there. When you update one SWF, After Effects calls to the new SWF and a re-rendered Quicktime shows the update. Moreover, SWFs are small in file size and could be e-mailed to the one machine which has After Effects on it (for big productions and several workers).

What feature in Adobe Flash would you most like to see added?
Better integration with sound. Animation is about timing. A second at 24 fps is 24 frames. But in Adobe Flash, sound sometimes becomes distorted, and long sounds that should be, say, 2880 frames long are a few frames off. If your sound is edited in the timeline of Flash, no one will notice that your 2880-frame animation is really 2875. But, if you edit the Flash video to an audio file, say from a Pro Tools®, you'll notice that the video is slightly faster. You'll either have to adjust the audio in Pro Tools or adjust the video in a video-editing program. You'll have to make adjustments with every tweak of video and tweak of audio. Post-production is a pain in the butt as it is, without making it more painful! Adobe needs to either fix the sound distortion or make editing sound in Adobe Flash professionally competitive with Pro Tools, so sound guys can work in Adobe Flash with the animators. Perhaps a bit of both.

Q & A WITH WYATT MILES

What do you do?

I mainly do character design and animation work right now, but I also really enjoy writing scripts, stories, poems, and books in my spare time. I'm very interested in using my abilities in animation and storytelling to create interactive media to teach children useful skills and good principles that will help them better their lives.

What's a typical day like for you?

For me, every day at work is different and exciting. Sometimes I'm animating a piece for a client, some days I'm designing characters, other days I'm writing and designing e-cards, and when I don't have any client work to do, I work on some of my own personal projects.

Describe the path that led you to where you are now.

I grew up in a large family of eight children. I was the third, and I learned to love kids and the way they think and interact with the world from my younger siblings. We loved making forts, creating games to play, watching cartoons, and playing outside. I believe it's my desire to hold onto my childhood memories and to stay in touch with my inner child that has led me to do what I'm doing today. I think there is still a child alive somewhere in all of us, and my greatest ambition in life is to be able to communicate with that part of people.

Who or what inspires you?

I grew up reading the newspaper comics. It was one of the great highlights of each day for me to sit down to a nutritious breakfast of Marshmallow Mateys and *Calvin and Hobbes*. I think it would be safe to say that Bill Watterson is the one person that has inspired me more than any other to become an artist. I fell in love with the world that he created for us with his wonderful talents and imagination and I hope that I can use my gifts to do something great as well. I am also very impressed with the love and respect that he has for his characters. There are very few artists who have preserved their characters as well as Watterson has.

Some of the other things that I fell in love with as a child that still inspire me today are Gary Larsen's *The Far Side*, all the Dr. Seuss books, Mercer Mayer's *Little Critter* books, *Winnie the Pooh*, and classical Disney movies, just to name a few.

I find things all around me that inspire me every day. This world is full of beautiful things and wonderful people. In general, it's the capacity of the human spirit in all of us to love, to laugh, to cry, to forgive, to learn, to grow, and to create beautiful things that fuels my passion for life and my work.

Last, but not least, is my family. Their love and support, I am certain, will see me through anything. My wife is my greatest love and my best friend in the whole world. Every day I get to spend with her brings new revelations and deeper meaning to my life. We have had one beautiful little girl together so far, and we hope to continue building our family.

Where do you see the future of your industry headed?

I'm generally a very optimistic person. I believe that we're going to see some more companies like Disney, Pixar, and Studio Ghibli come out of the woodwork and tell some fantastic stories that will inspire people and change the world. I believe that traditional hand-drawn animation will see a big resurgence in the mainstream market at some point, and I hope to be a part of that.

What suggestions do you have for someone wanting to enter your field?

Be ready for a lot of hard work. Animation and storytelling are extremely fun and rewarding, but like any other job it takes an incredible amount of discipline, hard work, and patience to become good at it. I have struggled for many years to acquire the small amount of skill I have as an artist and animator. I am going to need to work a lot more diligently if I'm going to be very successful.

Also, I would suggest learning to live very frugally. Artists are not generally wealthy people, and even if, by some miracle, you happen to strike it rich, it will only be after many years of poverty-line subsistence. Read the life histories of some of the most successful artists if you want to get a better idea of what artists go through.

What do you like most about your job?

The freedom; I live a very extraordinary life where I make my own schedule. I have been able to spend more time with my family than most men have the chance to. I don't make much money, but the freedom I enjoy has allowed me to make a lot of wonderful memories with my family that I will treasure forever.

With the independence I enjoy as a freelance artist/animator, however, comes the temptation to slack off at times. It takes a great amount of self-discipline to do freelance work successfully. It has been an uphill battle for me, but I feel like I am beginning to win. I like a good challenge and I certainly get that with my work.

What do you like least about your job?
The financial management; it is an extremely tedious thing for me to manage money and finances. If I ever make any significant money with my work, the first thing I will do is hire someone to manage it for me. Yuck!!

What are you working on now?
I'm working on another game with PlayFirst® headed by Dave Gilbert of Wadget Eye Studios. I can't say what it is right now, but it will be coming out soon. I worked with them on a previous title as well, called "Emerald City Confidential' which is a game based on the world of Oz. We had a lot of fun working on that one. Dave is an amazing creative talent. Check out his work at www.wadjeteyegames.com.

I'm also working on some e-cards for a company called RazorSight.

In my spare time, I'm working on a board book for children that I hope to have published soon.

If you work with Adobe Flash, what's a tip or trick in Adobe Flash that you'd like to share with others?
I love to find ways to combine elements of what Adobe® Photoshop® and Adobe® Illustrator® can do into Flash. Something very simple that a friend once showed me, but that I haven't had a lot of time to play around with yet, is that you can import .png pieces into an Adobe Flash file and use them to create animations. I always knew that this was possible, but what I did not know was that you can double-click on the .png elements in your Library and select the option **Allow smoothing**. This solves that problem of ugly pixilation that you usually get with photo elements when they are displayed at anything other than 100% on your stage. What does this mean? It means you can create awesome animations in Adobe Flash that don't look like typical Adobe Flash animations!

Here is a link to the one animation I've done so far using this method: www.flashpotatoes.com/Sample/cut_out.html

What feature in Adobe Flash would you most like to see added?
I would like it if they would make it possible to add filter effects to Graphic symbols. The reason for this is that I have used the Movie Clip filters in creating animations that needed to be exported as .png sequences. Since the animation

contained within Movie Clips will not play when exported this way, you have to make each frame of an effects sequence into a separate Movie Clip. It's not a huge deal, but it would save me some time.

INDEX

A

Alpha, 149
Animatic
    explained, 139–141
    timing, 13
Animation
    approach, 14
    defined, 159
    keyframe, 224–226
    pose-to-pose, 161
    principles, 160–166
    rough, 167
    straight ahead, 161
    testing, 132–133
Anticipation, 161
Appeal, 166
Arcs, 163
Aspect ratio, 17
Audio
    editing, 156–157
    embedded, 232
    record, 13
    importing, 14
    properties, 232–233
    waveform, 141–142

B

Background
    design, 90–91
    layout, 98, 100
    reusing, 98–99

Bandwidth profiler, 234–236
Bitmaps
    importing, 60–61
    textures, 124–129

C

Camera
    angles defined, 78–82
    recreating movements, 144–154
Characters
    back story, 6
    design, 12–13, 87–90
    rigging, 117–119
Cinematography, 109–110, 138–139
Color
    mixer, 53–55
    theory, 111–114
Comments, 142
Composition, 93–98
Compression
    of sound, 232–233
    of video, 239–241
Contour, 37

D

Delivery, 15, 229
Design
    graphic, 86–87
    sound, 15
    two-dimensional, 93–98

Dialogue
  animating, 176
  writing, 77
Distribution, 243
Drag and follow-through, 162
Drawing
  principles, 36–40
  tools, 40–53

E
Easing, 147, 163
Editing
  audio hardware, 11
  clips, 241–242
Edit Multiple Frames, 193–194
Equipment, 9–11
Eraser, 53
Exaggeration, 165
Exporting
  from a Mac, 239–240
  from a PC, 240–241
Expression sheet, 123–124
Eyedropper tool, 47

F
Files
  naming convention, 16–17
  preparation, 17–20
File size
  reducing, 230–231
Fill, 45, 50–51
Film festivals, 244
Filters
  applying a bevel, 220
  applying a blur, 132
  applying a drop shadow, 195
  applying a glow, 195–196
  how to create, 132
Folder structure, 16, 24, 115–116
Foreshortening, 36
Frame rate
  film vs. web, 17
  setting, 19–20

G
Gradients, 55–57
Guidelines, 121–122
Guide layer, 170
Graphic symbol
  converting to, 102, 126

H
Hand tool, 53
Handles, 43, 50
Hardware, 9–11

I
Ink bottle, 45

K
Keyboard shortcuts, 31–34
Keyframe
  adjusting position, 131
  defined, 34–35
  deleting, 104
  duplicating, 145
  extending along timeline, 143
  inserting, 131
  previewing animation, 131
  types of, 146

L
Layers
  how to use, 59
  distributing to, 103–104
  properties, 153
Library
  assembling, 114–116
  cleaning, 231–232
Line tool, 41

M
Masks
  animating, 154
  applying shape hints to, 217–219
  creating, 151–153
  examined, 214–217
  previewing, 215

Model Sheet, 122–123
Modify, 34, 50–52, 102, 120, 218, 230
Motion Guide, 169–171
Motion Tween
    applied to different layers, 147
    how to create, 146–147
    with rotation, 168–169
Movieclip
    compared to a graphic symbol, 148

N
Nesting symbols, 171–176
Networking, 242–243

O
Onion Skin Tool, 160, 163, 167
Optimizing
    files, 229–232
    audio, 232–233
    files for web, 234–238
Overlapping
    drawing principle, 36
    objects, 46
    action, 162

P
Paint bucket, 45, 47
Panels, 20–22
Pencil tool, 41, 43–44, 50
Perspective, 39, 65
Promotion, 242
Properties Panel
    advanced tab, 129
    color tab, 129
    elements, 19
    instance names, 107–108
    opacity setting, 149
    orient to path, 171
    polystar, 58
    rotation, 168
Publish settings, 234–236

Q
Quicktime, 239–241

R
Raster art, 28, 124
Reference, 3, 7, 92–93
Reverse frames, 202–204
Rulers, 120–122

S
Scale, 62, 146
Scenes
    defined, 16
    setting up, 139–141
Script, 74–77
Secondary action, 164
Selection tool, 41
Shading, 38–39
Shapes, 57–58
Shape Hints, 217–219
Shape Tween, 169
Silhouette, 12–13, 38, 87–88, 95
Sketching
    ideas, 114
    on location, 92–93
    people, 12
    scenes, 98
    styles, 89
    with the brush tool, 40, 49
Sound
    defined, 154–155
    editing, 156–157
    effects, 15, 138
Special effects, 177–227
Squash and stretch, 160
Stage dimensions, 17, 19, 27, 34
Staging, 13, 99, 139, 161
Story
    getting ideas, 1–5, 7
    types, 67–69
    elements of, 70–74

Storyboard
  defined, 13
  elements of, 135–138
  template, 138, 158
Stroke, 43–46
Subselection tool, 43
.swf, 132
Symbols
  converting to, 126
  nesting, 171–176
  and their meanings, 91

T
Test movie, 132
Timeline
  defined, 34
  previewing with the scrubber bar,
    131
Timing
  along the timeline, 143
  in film, 228
  your animation, 164
Tools
  drawing, 40–53
  shortcuts, 40
  transform, 62–63
Type, 52

V
Vector art, 27–28
Visual development, 12, 85–87

W
Walkcycles, 166
Workflow
  production process, 12–15
Workspace, 20–23